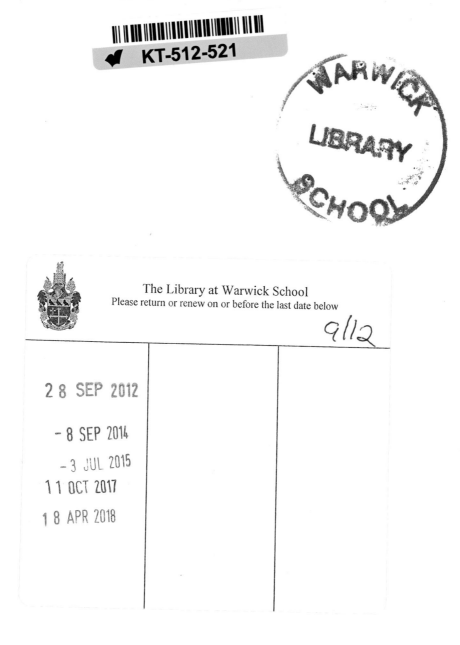

AFTER THE
ARAB SPRING

AFTER THE
ARAB SPRING

HOW ISLAMISTS HIJACKED
THE MIDDLE EAST REVOLTS

JOHN R. BRADLEY

palgrave
macmillan

First published in 2012 by PALGRAVE MACMILLAN® in the United
States—a division of St. Martin's Press LLC, 175 Fifth Avenue, New
York, NY 10010.

Where this book is distributed in the UK, Europe and the rest of the
world, this is by Palgrave Macmillan, a division of Macmillan Publishers
Limited, registered in England, company number 785998, of Houndmills,
Basingstoke, Hampshire RG21 6XS.

Palgrave Macmillan is the global academic imprint of the above
companies and has companies and representatives throughout the world.

Palgrave® and Macmillan® are registered trademarks in the United
States, the United Kingdom, Europe and other countries.

ISBN 978-0-230-33819-7

Library of Congress Cataloging-in-Publication Data

Bradley, John R., 1970–
    After the Arab spring : how Islamists hijacked the Middle East revolts /
John R. Bradley.
        p.   cm.
    Includes index.
    ISBN 978-0-230-33819-7 (hardback)
    1. Middle East—Politics and government—21st
century.   2. Revolutions—Middle East.   3. Islam and politics—Middle
East.   4. Democratization—Middle East.   I. Title.
DS63.18.B73   2012
956.05'4—dc23

                                                                2011040890

A catalogue record of the book is available from the British Library.

Design by Letra Libre, Inc.

First edition: January 2012

10   9   8   7   6   5   4   3   2   1

Printed in the United States of America.

CONTENTS

INTRODUCTION

AN ARAB SPRING?

MY HEART SANK WHEN NEWS BROKE THAT A POPULAR UPRISING HAD erupted in Tunisia. It was not that I harbored any sympathy for the country's strongman, Zine El-Abidine Ben Ali, who had been in power for more than two decades. I had still less for his extended family, which had robbed the country blind. Thousands of Tunisians had poured into the streets, and I knew why.

But while most Western reporters considered unrest in the Middle East a step in the direction of democracy, I thought the opposite. It is the Islamists, who wish to create Islamic states and impose Islamic law, who will emerge triumphant from the present chaos.

What happened in Tunisia, the center of the Arab Spring, was repeated throughout the Middle East.

The country was ruled by the most secular Arab regime and was the most socially liberal and progressive Muslim country in the Middle East. As such, before its revolution it had been the last bulwark against the Saudi-funded Wahhabi form of Islam that, since the oil boom of the 1970s, had spread everywhere else in the Islamic world.

Tunisia's revolution was spontaneous and lacked any kind of ideological underpinning. Bearded zealots played little, if any, part in the uprising. They were certainly not its driving force. That would be typical of all the Arab revolts, apart from in Libya, at least in their initial stages. In Tunisia, there was a reason that the Islamists were not the vanguard: for decades the regime had imprisoned or exiled them.

However, their hijacking of the revolution did not mark the first time in history that such an upheaval took a disastrous turn. It often happens that the revolutionaries who sacrificed themselves are then dismayed to see their hopes dashed while a new order that is as bad as, if not worse than, the one they ousted becomes reality. The modern era's most popular revolutions offer depressing precedents. The French Revolution led to the Great Terror, the Russian Revolution led to the nightmare of Stalin, and the Iranian Revolution led to the tyrannical rule of the mullahs. The last example is particularly relevant. The 1979 Iranian uprising is the only true revolution (as opposed to military coups) in modern Middle Eastern history. Tunisia's Islamists were a minority among the population at large, and they were very much in the infancy of their campaign when the popular uprising started in December 2010. But so were the Iranian mullahs in the early stages of the Iranian Revolution in the 1970s, yet they exploited the postrevolutionary chaos to seize control.

If that were to happen in Tunisia, what lay in store for the wider region? A failed transition to democracy in the most progressive Arab country would bode ill for the possibility of success elsewhere. From Morocco to Yemen, Saudi Arabia to Egypt, secularism and liberalism were already anathema. Wahhabi-inspired Islam already had a firm foothold. Syria, the only ostensibly secular Arab country apart from Tunisia, was ruled by a minority Shia cult, and there, too, the Sunni fundamentalist Muslim Brotherhood was ready to pounce.

Tunisia is little known in the West. Sandwiched between resource-rich neighbors Algeria and Libya, under Ben Ali it had been stubbornly isolationist and mostly stayed out of the region's turbulent politics. Tight restrictions were placed on the foreign media and international human rights organizations: another reason it was not much covered. But even fellow Arabs rarely gave it a second thought, aside from sex-starved Algerian and Libyan men who escaped their stifling societies by descending on the Tunisian capital's vibrant nightlife. For Americans, Tunisia was completely off the radar; Britons knew it only as an affordable, nearby holiday destination. After the revolution, most Western journalists who descended on Tunisia had therefore previously had little reason or opportunity to visit; but before they could get acquainted with its uniqueness, they were rushed off to Egypt to cover the follow-on revolution there.

Much of the excited coverage of Ben Ali's ouster willfully misrepresented Tunisia's modern history, caricaturing the regime as on a par with other brutally oppressive Arab dictatorships. That was not the reality. Unfamiliarity, too, accounted for an immediate championing of the Tunisian uprising as a thirst for democracy, both within the country and throughout the region.

Constant parallels were drawn to the fall of the Berlin Wall and to the end of Communism. Pluralism, tolerance, and free expression, we were told, would finally blossom in this apparently cruelly repressive country, its rich pollen inexorably carried through the Middle East.

When the Western media gets an idea like this into its head, it tends to steamroll. Then it turns into a self-fulfilling prophecy. Few pundits then want to risk alienating their readers and viewers by going out on a limb. I saw firsthand the consequences of doing so when, after Egyptian dictator Hosni Mubarak resigned in February 2011, I appeared on an American news network—having written a book, *Inside Egypt: The Land of the Pharaohs on the Brink of a Revolution* (2008), that predicted the Cairo uprising. We marveled at the million-strong crowd celebrating in the capital's Tahrir Square. However, after I warned of an Islamist takeover in the not-too-distant future, the interview abruptly ended. This was a night, the presenter told me, for celebration. Nobody wanted to hear my doom and gloom, and I was thanked and summarily sent away.

Nobody benefits from such sentimentality.

As Middle Eastern pundits continued their joyous Arab Spring narrative, I did manage to publish a number of articles that warned this Tunisian tsunami would leave in its wake a catastrophic new reality.[1] Tunisia itself would fall to the Islamists, not through elections but by violent intimidation on the ground. That would mean, I argued, the end of decades of progressive and modern social policies for the Tunisian people. It would also sound the death knell for resistance to fanatical Wahhabi-style Islam in the Middle East.

For all its history of isolationism, Tunisia was suddenly an Arab country of crucial significance, but for reasons few wanted to discuss. In George Orwell's novel *1984, political* repression is accompanied by *social* freedom. The Proles are allowed to lead lives of drunken sexual license as long as they do not threaten the party. In vaguely the same way, the secularist Tunisian regime had tolerated liberties unheard-of in other Arab countries. It did so as a matter of principle, not expediency. It had been governed by a well-oiled francophone bureaucracy, ruled by a regime that embraced secularism with a passion and loathed Islamist ideology. This was an authoritarian Muslim country where abortion was legal, where schools taught sex education, and where the veil was banned in government institutions (and severely discouraged elsewhere).

Since gaining independence in 1956, Tunisia had been the undisputed champion of women's rights in the Muslim world. Polygamy had been outlawed for decades. Uniquely in the Middle East, the Tunisian army was given no role in politics, and the education system was allocated more funding than the defense budget. When the uprising broke out, the Tunisian education system was world class, ranking seventeenth globally in terms of overall quality and seventh in math and science.[2]

The Tunisian regime was not driven by a need to morally subjugate the people, which is what drives the Islamists. It was solely driven by the wish to retain power. It achieved this not through brutal repression, as the world has come to believe, but rather by dramatically increasing the living standards of the middle class. In return for a commitment to investing in their future, the Tunisian regime demanded political acquiescence. Personal freedoms and development were enthusiastically encouraged, while clear red lines demarcated political and religious expression. The historic argument of the regime was that, in the chaos and vulnerability of newly independent societies, stability is imperative if progress is to be achieved. This social contract, loosely based on the Singapore model of governance, broke down, as the opening chapter shows, because of a severe economic downturn and increasing evidence of widespread corruption among Ben Ali's extended family, not because of a lack of democracy.

By virtue of its pervasive, state-encouraged liberalism, Tunisia had always been reviled by the Islamists as a veritable cesspool of Westernization. That was why, during my two decades of often extended visits, I had grown to love the country, having nothing but loathing for religious extremism of whatever creed. My first trip to Tunisia had been during a university vacation in the early 1990s, when the regime was beginning to imprison or exile the country's minority Islamists. They were accused of planning violent attacks on government institutions and foreigners, or scheming for the overthrow of the secular state to impose strict Islamic law. There had indeed been a number of terrorist attacks in the country in the lead-up to their arrest, though whether the authorities arrested the real culprits remains anyone's guess. But note that they were exiled or imprisoned, not "disappeared." In contrast to every other country in the region, there is no clear evidence that the Tunisian regime murdered any of its political opponents. Ben Ali, in fact, had seized power in 1997 in large part because of his disgust at a decision by the president, Habib Bourguiba, to execute a group of alleged Islamist terrorists, despite Ben Ali's own hatred of everything the Islamists stood for. In the end, the alleged terrorists were not executed.

Even before Ben Ali had boarded a plane for his own permanent exile—ironically, it would land in the Wahhabi heartland of Saudi Arabia—Tunisia's Islamist rabble-rousers were furiously plotting their ascent.

In the name of democracy, the postrevolutionary interim government had released them en masse from prison and invited the others home from exile. Given their freedom, they quickly set about imposing stricter religious social mores. Amidst the chaos of postrevolutionary Tunisia, Islamist moral police were prowling the streets seeking converts and castigating unveiled women for their lack of modesty. There was no official organization that took responsibility for the actions, just groups of young men who had taken it upon themselves to radicalize society from below—and with such enthusiasm that it seemed they had been waiting all their lives for the opportunity. All women, they demanded, must don the veil. They firebombed houses of ill repute. In broad daylight, they stabbed a liberal artist in the head. Tunisia, they chanted, was now an Islamist state.

The Islamists were taking over more quickly than I had anticipated, and it was heartbreaking.

THE TUNISIAN AND EGYPTIAN REVOLUTIONS were hailed as templates for the rest of the Arab world. However, such revolutions should be judged not by their intentions but by their outcomes.

The story of postrevolutionary Tunisia and Egypt, as told in the opening chapters of this book, is far more instructive.

The world's attention quickly moved on to the next theater of the extraordinary, fast-moving drama. Tunisia was relegated back to obscurity. The rise of radical Islamism in Egypt was glossed over, too, in the increasingly scant coverage that country received. However, there was one constant, the phrase "Arab Spring," touted as though we were witnessing an unambiguous leap forward for the Arabs. Their cultures, we were told, were at last united and marching forward in the name of achieving democracy.

This was self-delusional, like the Western elite's championing of Francis Fukuyama's theory in the early 1990s of the end of history following the fall of the Berlin Wall.

Now leading Western politicians and commentators similarly proclaim that oppressed Arab peoples are rising up against tyranny because of a yearning for the classic Western liberal values of tolerance and representative government. A common humanity, they insist, is manifested in their collective embrace of Western-defined human rights and free expression. No sane person wants to be arrested and tortured for speaking his or her mind, whether they are in Riyadh or Austin, Texas. However, different peoples of different cultures and religions who speak different languages do not, by default, instinctively translate their wish to live with dignity into a love of the British parliamentary system or American individualism. To suggest otherwise, as many armchair commentators do, is crude and simplistic.

The slogans written in English on the demonstrators' placards did give the West cause for hope, as did some Westernized revolutionaries who tweeted their commentary in English. English-speaking demonstrators were eagerly sought out by Western television crews, many without translators and aware of an aversion among their producers to the use of subtitles. The placards, tweets, and commentaries of the English-speaking elite would prove, though, a poor proxy for the vox populi. For the Arab masses, the chief grievance was not a lack of political freedom, but of jobs. A longing for democracy has little resonance even in Tunisia or Egypt, the only two countries, at the time of writing, that have managed to topple their dictators without the help of Western military intervention.

Habib Bourguiba, who ruled Tunisia with an iron fist from 1956 until 1987, was—and remains—deeply loved by the Tunisian masses, despite his autocracy. While many of Ben Ali's residences were pillaged during the revolution, a monument to Bourguiba in his hometown, Monastir, which witnessed extensive looting and vandalism, was left unscathed. A few months later, Tunisians were proudly celebrating the official holiday marked in Bourguiba's honor, happy that they could sing his praises because the event was no longer tightly stage-managed as it had been during the rule of Ben Ali (for whom there could be only one star in the sky). When Islamists, who had been persecuted by Bourguiba, held a rally in Bourguiba's hometown and things turned chaotic, even they pacified the hostile crowd by heaping praise on the country's first independence leader.[3] After Ben Ali fled, as an attempt to take wind out of the sails of young revolutionaries rioting in the streets in protest at remnants of the old regime remaining in power, the octogenarian Beji Caid Essebsi was dragged out of retirement and appointed interim prime minister. One would think that the revolutionaries would oppose a member of the old guard. But no: they largely left the streets. Essebsi was a veteran of the Bourguiba government. By default, he therefore won the trust of almost everyone—as much as anyone could have under the circumstances.

Egypt's Gamal Abdel Nasser, brought to power in the 1952 coup that overthrew the British-backed monarchy, also relentlessly cracked down on free speech and outlawed political opposition. He never allowed free elections during the two decades of his rule. But his portrait was held aloft by the masses during the 2011 Egyptian revolution, and it remains difficult to find an ordinary Egyptian who will say a word against him. A major opinion poll after the Egyptian revolution found that, even among the revolutionaries themselves, only 19 percent of respondents said a desire for democracy was a top motivation for toppling Mubarak. Some 65 percent instead pinpointed the state of the economy.[4]

Why are these two authoritarian, undemocratic leaders still so revered?

Over the decades, I have asked that question more times than I care to remember in both countries. Tunisians and Egyptians have invariably offered the same explanation. Neither leader was personally corrupt. Both respected the dignity of their people. And, during their rule, it was not difficult to bring bread to the table. Their dictatorial tendencies do not enter into the discussion. Likewise, their diametrically opposed foreign policies seem to be of little importance: Nasser was steadfastly anti-imperialist, while Bourguiba rejected Nasser's pan-Arabism and forged close ties with the West.

It is, then, somewhat paradoxical that Tunisia should have been the catalyst for revolutionary upheaval in Egypt and uprisings elsewhere in the Arab world. Tunisians do not have much love for Egyptians especially. I have always found their response to my distinctive Egyptian dialect decidedly lukewarm. Tunisians I have spoken to have mostly considered Egyptians inveterate tricksters and hypocritical for their ostentatious, but often superficial, displays of piety. In turn, Egyptians considered Tunisia's ban on the veil, and its legalized red-light districts, as utter madness. This reality soon undermined all the talk of Arab brotherly love between the two countries in the wake of the Arab Spring. A few months after the Tunisian and Egyptian revolutions, the two countries faced off in a soccer match in Cairo. Following a disputed decision by the referee, the Egyptian crowd broke into a riot, invaded the playing field, and attacked the Tunisian players.[5] I happened to be in Tunis that evening. It was not an easy place to be ordering a coffee in my Egyptian accent.

So the idea that the Arab uprisings represented a revival of Nasser's pan-Arabism, like so many of the theories promoted by Middle East experts, was wishful thinking.

Indeed, I was struck, as I flew back and forth between post-revolutionary Tunisia and Egypt, by the contempt ordinary people in both countries showed for Libyans as their country descended into civil war. Egyptians were under the misguided impression that all Libyans were, as they thought all Saudis were, filthy rich, so they could not for the life of them understand why they had taken up arms. Tunisians have always despised Libyans, so much so that it makes their coolness toward Egyptians seem like smoldering passion. For Tunisians, Libyans were dumb Bedouins. Soon they were violently attacking refugee camps set up for Libyans in the Tunisian south.[6]

IT IS A FUNDAMENTAL MISTAKE to view the Middle East revolts through the rose-tinted prism of either pan-Arab or Western ideals. But an even greater error is to assume that democracy, even in the event that it does eventually triumph, will be an enemy of Islamism. In the Arab world, when the gift of democracy is unwrapped, it is the Islamists who spring out of the box.

Extremist Islamists are despised by most Muslims, as is often pointed out by observers of the region. However, that observation misses a crucial point. In Arab countries, only between 20 and 40 percent of the population votes in local and national elections. And that pattern looks set to continue. In Egypt's first free election, in March 2011, for a referendum on a new constitution, only 41 percent of eligible voters made their way to the polling booths. In Tunisia, when the initial deadline for voter registration passed in mid-August 2011, only 16 percent of the country's eligible voters had made the effort.[7]

Given this, it is by no means impossible for the Islamists to secure a majority from the minority. The reason is simple: Their supporters are the most fanatical, so they turn out in larger numbers to vote. And the Islamists are always more successful at getting them to vote. In Tunisia, the initial deadline for voter registration was extended by a month. The Islamists then launched a recruit-ment drive centered on the faithful attending Ramadan evening prayers in the mosques. It was their persuasive arguments, among their electoral base and on their home turf, that largely accounted for the eventual increase in total voter registration to around 50 percent of those eligible to cast a ballot.[8] Of course, in Tunisia there will not be a 100 percent turnout in future elections. In Oc-tober 2011, in its first free and fair elections to elect a consultative chamber to draft a new constitution, only half of all eligible voters cast their vote. The Islamists triumphed.

About 30 percent of the population was routinely reported by pollsters to have supported the Islamists in Tunisia and Egypt before the revolutions. This strikes me as an underestimate. Yet given the mathematics of elections, this is still a terrifying statistic. If the turnout for an election is 50 or even 60 percent, and most of the Islamists vote, it means they will get at least half the seats in parliament. In both countries, according to the systems in place at the time of writing, that would be enough to gain the power of veto and introduce laws from scratch.

The Islamists, to put it simply, do not need majority support from the total population to triumph in elections. They need a majority within the minority who vote. Still, in both Tunisia and Egypt, they are playing a deft game of standing only for half of the seats up for grabs to calm fears of an immediate takeover. For them, the long term is what matters. Elections are a necessary evil, but at the same time useful, providing cover for more radical change, at a much swifter pace, on the ground. The Western me-dia can be relied on to quote "moderate" stances adopted by the leaders of Islamist groups and to highlight their lack of a clear majority as evidence that they have failed to hijack the revolutions, when in fact the Islamists have deliberately planned to stand in only a minority of seats and their pro-democracy rhetoric masks a darker reality. When, in time, they do decide to stand for all the available seats, gaining a majority from within a minority will be their aim, as it is for all parties in the first-past-the-post democratic systems, whether or not religious extremism plays a part.

Consider Britain, the oldest Western democracy.

The prime minister at the time of the Arab Spring, David Cameron, was elected in 2010 with 36 percent of the total vote. Even that did not represent his support among the total population, because only 65 percent of eligible British voted. And there are millions of unregistered Britons, and many are not eligible to cast a ballot (prisoners, for example). So Cameron, who was busy promoting democracy in the Middle East as the catch-all solution to its myriad problems and conflicts, himself had the demonstrable support of only perhaps 15 percent of the total voting-age British population.

BUT WHATEVER THE THEORY of what democratization will bring to the new Arab world, the history before the uprisings began is crystal clear. Where democracy, however tentatively, was introduced, it was the Islamists who benefited.

Democracy came to Morocco, and the fundamentalist Peace and Justice Party increased its number of seats at each election. It is only a matter of time before it forms a majority in parliament. Democracy came to Gaza, and the extremist Islamist group, Hamas, took power. In Bahrain, in the wake of democratic reforms a decade before the Arab Spring, a Sunni-dominated block hell-bent on banning alcohol took control of the elected chamber (despite Bahrain being 60 percent Shia and historically one of the most liberal Arab countries). The same is true of Yemen: The ruling party's main opposition in parliament is drawn from the Islamist Islah (Reform) movement. Hezbollah, the Shia resistance party, controls the Lebanese parliament. In Egypt, the Muslim Brotherhood was officially outlawed during dictator Hosni Mubarak's thirty-year rule, but in 2005 the group won a quarter of the parliamentary seats by running as independents.

This book illustrates why the Arab Spring, rather than ushering in a period of liberalism and pluralism for the region, has accelerated this reactionary Islamist trend.

Arabs are not, of course, somehow genetically or culturally incapable of embracing representative democracy. Rather, the reason the Islamists will triumph is a fluke of circumstance. With the exception of Tunisia and Syria, secular regimes throughout the Middle East had, since the 1980s, cultivated Islamist political groups as a way of deflecting popular anger at the regimes' close alliance with the West, which in turn was blamed by the masses for keeping the regimes in power through military and political support. This cultivation of nonviolent Islamist groups marginalized liberal figures, who were simultaneously intimidated by the Islamist conservatives and persecuted by the regimes. The Islamists benefited because their goal is always to Islamize society from below, not to overthrow the existing order. The regimes benefited because, in addition to marginalizing liberal, pro-democracy forces, they could use the rise of the Islamists as an implicit threat to the West: it is either us or the Islamists. This kept calls in Washington for speedier reforms at a whisper.

What nobody had bargained for was a wave of revolutionary upheaval at a time when the liberals were so cowered, persecuted, and unpopular that they did not have a chance of filling the resulting vacuum. The Islamists, though, were organized and disciplined, and, while never likely to instigate revolution, sure were eager to exploit the consequences. When the revolutions in Tunisia and Egypt failed to overthrow the old regimes, instead achieving only pyrrhic victories in ousting the heads of state, this old alliance—between the reactionary old guard and the Islamists—was further cemented, while the liberals were further marginalized. This became the dominant pattern throughout the Arab Spring. After tribal and sectarian tensions were brought to the surface, and America decided to back a Saudi-led counterrevolution in favor of the status quo, whatever stand there had been in favor of freedom and pluralism was swept off its feet under the avalanche of more reactionary forces.

ONE

THE DEATH OF TUNISIA'S SECULARISM

I HAD BARELY HAD A CHANCE TO SIP MY CAFÉ AU LAIT BEFORE THE tear-gas canisters started whizzing over our heads. Grimacing waiters piled up the tables and chairs from the sidewalk: yet another day's business lost. I scrambled for cover. In an instant, the Tunisian capital's main boulevard, Habib Bourguiba Avenue, had filled with jeering, whistling rioters pouring in from the side streets. Thick lines of black-clad antiriot police moved to disperse them. It was two months since the revolution had ousted longtime strongman Ben Ali. An interim regime, mostly made up of the old guard, were busy entrenching their political power, while the previously marginalized Islamists were taking over the streets. The regular police had retreated to their stations, leaving the once tranquil capital city a lawless free-for-all.

Habib Bourguiba Avenue is home to the interior ministry and other key government ministries. It is the most beautiful street in the Arab world, a mélange of nineteenth-century French neoclassical buildings and others built in the Arabic style along-side 1960s modernist banks and offices. Now half of it was per-manently cordoned off by barbed wire and tanks. In the absence of regular police, the army had taken over securing the down-town area. Soon the soldiers were backing up riot police, firing shots into the air. The soldiers had no training in crowd control. Uniquely in the Arab world, they had been given no role in poli-tics—something that would prove crucial in the dictator's down-fall. They had adopted a crude crowd-dispersal strategy: shout like a madman as a first verbal warning, then fire once into the air. If that did not clear the protestors, they shot three more times into the air. As a last resort they shoved their weapons into the chests of the rebellious young men. Riot police finally dragged the pro-testors into armored vans with a liberal volley of kicks and slaps.

The riot that I was caught up in that evening was caused by a number of youth groups. Locals took cover as young men at-tacked each other. The main group was drawn from the dem-onstrators camped outside the National Theater: a few hundred revolutionary die-hards protesting about the reestablishment of figures from the former regime after the president was ousted, as well as continuing lack of freedoms and elections and economic reform. In a city of some 2 million, these demonstrators never numbered more than a few hundred, and local business owners had grown to hate them. Every so often something would spark their ire, a riot would ensue, and the store owners would be forced to pull down their shutters.

I made my way into a side street eager to get back to my little budget hotel. But many of the rioters had been hemmed in there.

Rival gangs of young men were beating the hell out of each other. More shots were fired into the air by the soldiers. More tear gas rained down on them. Again the demonstrators dispersed. In their wake I saw a man bleeding profusely from the head. I watched as a medical team arrived, declared him dead, and wrapped him in the white shroud of a martyr. For a moment the rioters, who had recongregated to witness the removal of the corpse, were united by their refocused anger and distress, and the entire downtown area was filled with a chorus of whistles. They had gotten it into their heads that it was the army, rather than one of their own rank and file, who had killed the young man. The owner of a little kiosk where I had taken refuge was as ignorant as everyone else as to what had really happened.

"*Hiya fawda,*" he told me. It's chaos.

On impulse I had videoed the events. Before what came to be known as Tunisia's Jasmine Revolution, the police would have rounded on me, too. Foreign correspondents were being closely observed, if granted permission to enter the country in the first place. Half an hour later, standing over a pool of blood that seeped into a sprinkling of sand, I asked myself: What did this young man die for? So that I and others could freely video his painful demise?

On my subsequent trips around Tunisia, I remembered this moment as one local after another asked me a variation on the same rhetorical question: "What use is freedom of speech and voting every five years if I can't feed my children?" Not that this young man's death even got reported. The foreign media, for whom Tunisia once again became irrelevant because it had lost its headline appeal, did not cover that evening's mayhem. But I was flabbergasted that even the local media ignored it. I searched in vain in the Arabic-language newspapers for three days for any kind of coverage. Editors who had once spouted praiseful Ben Ali propaganda mostly kept their jobs and threw their weight behind the interim regime[1]—just a watered-down version of what existed before the uprising but having no authority.

THE YOUNG RIOTERS' GRIEVANCES WERE LEGITIMATE. Nobody could deny that. Early on, it became clear that the revolution had not overthrown the old order. The former elite, after a little exercise in window dressing, once again consolidated its hold on power. The revolution had been an abysmal failure. It rid the country only of the regime's top layer.

But who would have expected anything else?

Crucially, the revolutionaries had not enjoyed the active support of the middle class, who had stayed at home during the uprising. And did the revolutionaries really believe that an elite that had spent five decades building the foundations of the modern Tunisian state were then going to hand over everything—the economy, the army, the education and health systems, the airports, the police force—unless forced to at the barrel of a gun? Least of all, perhaps, to a few dozen Facebook activists who had been among the most prominent groups of revolutionaries, and who tried to keep the revolutionary spirit alive after almost everyone had had abandoned hope of serious positive change. For all they were feted by the Western media, few in Tunisia knew who these revolutionaries were. Barely out of their teens, they had no experience to speak of, other than screaming slogans.

Worse, their blind enthusiasm for Western democracy—childishly egged on by supporters safe and secure in the West—was fundamentally flawed.

When the revolution broke out, the poverty rate in Britain was 20 percent, the same as it had been during the Victorian era, and some 40 million Americans were living on food stamps. In Tunisia, the poverty rate, according to the World Bank, was 4 percent.[2] So how was a rapid transition to democracy supposed to resolve overnight Tunisia's economic woes? Like Tunisia, both Britain and America were mired in their worst economic downturns in decades. Many of the governments of western Europe, too, were facing bankruptcy, heading cap in hand to the International Monetary Fund and World Bank. The masses there were facing the indignity of eking out a living in the face of massive youth unemployment and endless rounds of cruel austerity measures.

Some parts of Tunisia, as was often pointed out, were far more prosperous than others. The coastal cities had been developed at the expense of the industrial and agricultural hinterland. But compare Manhattan to downtown Detroit, the beachfronts of Florida with the impoverished farming towns of the Midwest. In the coverage of Tunisia's supposed economic mismanagement, which became the model for coverage of the rest of the Arab world, these comparisons were never made. Instead, journalists held tight to the myth that *we* had got everything right, while *they* wanted nothing more than to emulate our fine example.

How inconvenient that, within months of Tunisia's uprising, there would be mass rioting in cities throughout England. And how telling that, immediately after the revolution, some 20,000 Tunisians fled to Europe, where they are hated. Here was a truer story about how little faith they had in their country's future, revolution or no revolution, democracy or no. It also illustrated how starry-eyed was the understanding in Tunisia of the harsh economic and social realities on the other side of the Mediterranean that awaited them, if they did not drown trying to get there.

THE TUNISIAN REVOLUTION HAD BEEN SPONTANEOUS. It spread from the impoverished hinterland to the working-class suburbs of the main cities. But it had no agenda other than rage at the regime. After Ben Ali and his family fled came the question that always poses a greater challenge following revolutionary upheaval, in which a well-trained vanguard is not ready to seize power: What comes next?

The answer was pandemonium.

I found it difficult to believe that Tunis had been my favorite city for the best part of two decades. This was where I had escaped to from the cultural backwater Saudi Arabia and ever more reactionary Egypt. It was here that I would relax in an ambiance of sophisticated, laid-back modernity. On this, my first trip to postrevolutionary Tunis, I was reflecting, with increasing horror, on the downtown district's dramatic transformation.

Before the revolution, the absence of beggars, aside from a small group of children who stashed away their shoes to evoke more sympathy from tourists, had been extraordinary. Now the mentally ill, roaming aimlessly, relieved themselves in full view, and hungry kids stole the leftovers on the restaurants' outdoor tables. In the old days, few women among the promenaders had worn the veil, and most of those who had were older and married with children in tow or visitors from the conservative countryside. Now maybe one in three wore the headscarf—even in this, the most cosmopolitan part of town—with a small percentage even donning the full face-covering *niqab*. The garment is historically alien to this country's traditional secular culture. Any woman wearing it before the revolution would have been arrested and made to sign a pledge that she would not repeat the absurd act. Indeed, for decades, beautiful women in tight jeans and T-shirts had strolled this stretch without any fear of leers and gropes and insults from men, in stark contrast to the rest of the Arab world. Since the 1950s, women had been fully integrated into urban society. But in the chaos of a country now ruled by an unelected interim revolutionary regime making vague promises of future elections, a small army of bearded zealots were filling the vacuum. They prowled the streets with piles of the Quran under their arms, making it their business to remind these Westernized women of their supposed lack of modesty.

Among the nonproselytizing young men, too, the beard had made a comeback. It might fairly be described as a new fashion statement. Under the prerevolutionary regime, men who had wanted to grow a long, Islamic-style beard had been asked to get a license from the local police station. The deposed regime's perspective on the beard had been equal to that on the veil: a political manifestation of a religion that should properly be viewed as a private affair, expressed not in terms of ostentatious symbols but rather quiet good deeds. After an investigation proved that they had no links to Islamist political or terror groups, permission would be granted, in the form of a letter that could then be presented to police.

For decades the police politely looked the other way as boys and men cruised each other in full view of coffee-sipping local families. The latter accepted such goings-on without a second thought. There were no roundups of "deviants" here, as there had been in many other Arab countries. The regime refused to give in to an Islamist moral order. Sex scandals did not exist. For as long as anyone could remember, the main downtown movie theater in Tunis had served as a meeting place for gay sex. Most of the city's smaller cinemas showed soft porn. But after the revolution, all that was advertised there were trashy Hollywood flicks— as though that were a sign of cultural advancement. It was said that security guards, with powerful torches and menacing looks, doubled as morality police. They had taken with a vengeance to patrolling the cinemas' aisles, though there had been no change in the law.

Tunis had also been one of the safest cities on earth. Violent crime was so rare that, when it did occur, it was gossiped about for weeks. But few now ventured out after dark. The postrevolutionary downtown's side streets were no-go areas, occupied by drunks, drug dealers, muggers, and aggressive prostitutes. The suburbs were worse: completely lawless. The police were too cowed to risk carrying out even an occasional patrol. Taxi drivers refused to pick up customers and sped home as soon as the sun went down. Thousands of criminals had escaped from the country's jails during the upheaval, including countless Islamist radicals, but also murderers, rapists, and serial delinquents. But the previously law-abiding youth had also been let off the leash. There was no controlling, either, drunken youths with time on their hands and a warped sense of what it meant finally to be "free." After the interim regime unblocked the web, removing all restrictions and thus making it possibly the freest Internet in the world, the most popular pages among the famously tech-savvy young Tunisians were not pro-democracy or even news sites, but porn.[3] So much for the Twitter revolution. Compulsory reading classes in high schools, the norm for half a century, were meanwhile dropped. Subsidies given to local book publishers were withdrawn. Book sales were down—although, aside from titles on the revolution, Islamist political texts were suddenly flying off the shelves. Works by Said Qutb, considered the father of modern jihad, took pride of place in the display windows.[4]

By the time I arrived in Tunisia, its once vast middle class, which had shunned the uprising, had sunk into a collective depression. Many were openly stating what, at the height of the uprising, would have been considered sacrilege: The revolution was a terrible mistake. A friend from the tourist resort of Sousse bumped into me in the capital. He was desperately seeking a job after being laid off by a hotel where he had worked as a waiter. He summed up the mood among his compatriots. "Those who didn't have work before the revolution still have some hope, because for them things were bad before and so they've lost nothing," he told me. "Anyway, they don't want to admit that things are worse now. It's kind of a question of pride. Who wants to admit that they were wrong? But you won't find anyone who works in the tourism industry or owns a business who's happy."

Those who previously did not have work had perhaps lost nothing in the short term, I told him. But their chances of finding work in the future were now slimmer. Tourism revenue, which had been the lifeblood of the economy, was down more than half, and there were no signs of the droves of Europeans tourists who used to pack the beaches. The second pillar of the economy, foreign investment, had also crumbled; foreign investors always value stability more than democracy. The neglected south of the country, where revolutionary fervor had first erupted, had been entirely dependent on trade with neighboring war-torn Libya. Now its industries ground to a halt as Libya descended into civil war. The poverty rate had, in the space of a few months, shot up from 4 percent to 25 percent, and unemployment was now officially 40 percent.[5]

TO THE GROWING DISMAY of the Tunisian middle class, it was becoming clearer by the day that the kind of democracy to emerge in the coming years would mean fewer, not more, personal freedoms and economic disaster. In postrevolutionary Tunisia, only the Islamists were brimming with confidence. My last book, *Behind the Veil of Vice* (2010), was published a few months before the Jasmine Revolution. In it I had argued that while the Tunisian regime certainly had its faults, it also had many saving graces. The problem with blindly advocating sudden and radical change was that it would dramatically increase the influence of the Islamists:

"What the Tunisian government suppresses is straightforward political opposition that organizes outside of the official perimeters, which, of course, it sets, and that seeks to overthrow the existing order. That constriction of discourse cannot be unconditionally accepted, but the problem in condemning it at the present time is that the group most determined to bring about change is also the one it is most difficult to have any sympathy with: the Islamists. A few hundred of them languish in prison, having attempted to overthrow the secular order, and the threat they pose even in this staunchly secular country cannot be overestimated. The best place for Islamists who want to overthrow the Tunisian state is indeed the prison cell, where they might be persuaded to modify their ideas, and not least because the first thing they would do if they gained power is deprive everyone else (and especially women) of their treasured liberties faster than they can scream 'Allahu akbar!'"[6]

This is precisely what happened, as Nadia El Fani, a Tunisian film director, knows only too well. For the half century between independence and the revolution, she would have had no problem showcasing to her fellow Tunisians her latest documentary, *Neither God nor Master*. It boldly declares her atheism and disdain for radical Islam. She and other secular-minded intellectuals had been indulged by the regime, and Tunisia boasted the best art-house cinema industry in the region. Nothing was off limits, apart from the shenanigans of the ruling elite and the promotion of Islamism. In May 2011, during the premiere of *Neither God nor Master,* about a hundred extremist Islamists—screaming "Allahu akbar"—smashed through the glass doors of the capital's postmodernist AfricArt cinema. They attacked the audience and threatened a massacre if the screening continued.[7] Nouri Bouzid, another celebrated Tunisian director and critic of Islamist extremism, had already been stabbed in the head. He seemed so terrified of accusing Islamist radicals that in subsequent interviews he refused to point the finger directly at them.[8] His opponents were not so shy. A week later, a speaker at an Islamist rally called for Bouzid to be "shot with a Kalashnikov," a call that was reportedly met with cries of "Allahu akbar" from the assembled crowd.[9] During the months following Ben Ali's ouster, such incidents were occurring with alarming frequency. They constituted the story the Western media, hooked on the happy-clappy Arab Spring narrative, did not want to tell. Tunisia's rich secular legacy was being eroded, through violence. Islamist mores were now imposed on the country.

In Abdallah Guech Street, a few hundred meters from the main mosque in the heart of Tunis's old quarter, a red-light district had thrived since the nineteenth century. Here the Ottomans legalized (and regulated) prostitution, as they had in much of the rest of the Muslim world. Uniquely, though, in the Arab world, the tradition in Tunisia endured. Every one of the country's historic quarters boasted bordellos—even Kairouan, Islam's fourth holiest city after Mecca, Medina, and Jerusalem. In keeping with Tunisia's deep-rooted secularism and unprecedented championing of Muslim women's rights, the prostitutes carried cards issued by the Interior Ministry. They paid taxes like everyone else. And enjoyed—along with their clients—the full protection of the law. All changed with the Jasmine Revolution.

A few weeks after Ben Ali was overthrown, hundreds of Islamists raided Abdallah Guech Street armed with Molotov cocktails and knives. They torched the brothels, yelled insults at the prostitutes, and declared that Tunisia was now an Islamic state. As soldiers fired into the air to disperse them and helicopters hovered overhead, the Islamists won a promise from the interim government that the brothels would be permanently closed.[10] Effectively, that is what happened. A huge gate was erected at the entrance to the district. In the country's other cities, brothels were targeted as well. They were all permanently closed. There were simultaneous demonstrations throughout the country against the sale of alcohol. When a small group of secularists in the laid-back resort of Sousse held a demonstration against this Islamist agenda, the zealots violently attacked them.[11]

Suspected Islamists otherwise occupied themselves with slitting the throat of a Polish Catholic priest. It was the first such sectarian murder in modern Tunisian history and was condemned by the interim regime as an act by a "group of extremist terrorist fascists."[12] The country's minority Christians were said to be "fleeing the country" or moving "to safer locations after receiving threats from Islamists."[13] Anti-Semitic slogans could be heard outside Tunisia's main synagogue—this in a country with no history of overt persecution of its Jewish minority.[14] Islamist fanatics also set fire to a synagogue in Tunisia's southern Gabes region, damaging the Torahs inside the building.[15] They rampaged through the center of Tunis in protest at a teacher who had allegedly said something deemed insulting to the Prophet Muhammad,[16] and they caused widespread chaos by rioting to demand the previously banned veil be made compulsory.[17] Pop groups were "stopped from getting on stage to perform," music being to the Islamist mind-set a decadent Western import and therefore to be outlawed, and a "festival was even canceled in the south of the country" under pressure from Islamists.[18] In a move that encapsulates the way the revolution got rid of one repressive regime only to open the door for one at least as bad, and probably much worse, in the name of Islam, lawyers representing Islamist groups forced the interim regime to block all pornographic sites on the web again.[19]

All this was happening in a country where for decades Nietzsche's dictum that God is dead had been calmly considered in the universities as part of the history of ideas. The intellectual elite, who in contrast to the middle classes threw their support behind the revolution, complained of a lack of police protection. But the laconic policeman in charge at a local station, in response to a desperate plea by one of the AfricArt audience members for help after the Islamists had ransacked the place, rather hit the nail on the head.

"Ben Ali was protecting you, and you kicked him out," he reportedly said, and shrugged.[20]

CRITICS OF THE DEPOSED TUNISIAN REGIME often allege that its anti-Islamist agenda was a way of currying favor with the West. Women's rights and secularism were promoted, but in that way the regime could offer its feminist and modernist credentials to conceal from outsiders the reality that it was oppressing both men and women. There was an element of truth to this argument. What country—in the Arab world or the West—had not jumped on the bandwagon of the war on terror to vitiate civil liberties? But unlike other Arab regimes, which cultivated moderate Islamist groups as a way of deflecting popular anger from their pro-Western policies, the Tunisian regime never yielded an inch to them.

To understand the reality of Tunisia's secular society and its unflagging promotion of women's rights, we must instead look at the ideology of the father of modern Tunisia.[21] On the bronze door to Habib Bourguiba's mausoleum in Monastir, the town where he was born in 1903 and died in 2000, is written:

THE SUPREME COMBATANT
THE LIBERATOR OF WOMEN
THE BUILDER OF MODERN TUNISIA

The political model adopted by Bourguiba as "the builder of modern Tunisia" posited that newly independent nations, often emerging from decades of upheaval, must restrict political participation and freedom of expression during the early years of nation building. It gave priority instead to the short-term goal of national security and raising economic quality of life, above freedom of political expression. Precedence was always given to the collective material good. But it is as the "liberator of women" that Bourguiba is best remembered. The feminism he championed encouraged women's independence, autonomy, and equality, in light of progressive Islamic thinking that sought to marry Islam with modernity. It came in conjunction with a kind of sexual revolution unprecedented in the Arab world or on the African continent.

Bourguiba's campaign for full female emancipation was launched in the form of a new Personal Status Code, which became law within months of independence in 1956. It outlawed polygamy, redefined marriage as a voluntary contract that conferred rights upon the wife as well as the husband, and set a minimum age for marriage.[22] It made mandatory the consent of the bride. It outlawed "the traditional practice of selling young girls, and underscoring the modern concept of marriage as a bond between two individuals rather than an alliance between two families."[23] Bourguiba simultaneously launched a family planning campaign, unusual by Western standards of the time. It focused on advocating birth control. In 1966, Tunisia became the first (and at the time of writing remains the only) Muslim country to make abortion available on demand.[24] According to a *Wall Street Journal* report in 2003, the aim was to use the declining birthrate to make personal and economic improvement:

> The government spends about $10 million each year to teach citizens about family planning and dispense birth-control devices to the remotest corners of a country nearly the size of Florida. Tunisia has gone a long way toward educating its women and bringing them into the work force. Men and schoolchildren learn about contraception. Mobile clinics offer free pap smears and breast exams. Tunisia has even persuaded its religious leaders to loosen their interpretation of the Quran to fit the cause.[25]

The result: a fertility rate of 2.08 before the revolution, compared to 7.2 in the 1960s. Life expectancy in Tunisia increased to above seventy-four years. Schooling and health care were free, and despite attempts in the postrevolutionary era to rewrite history, the reality was that they were excellent. High literacy rates helped a third of Tunisian youths to enter university, where women made up 60 percent of the students. What is perhaps most remarkable is that Bourguiba achieved this radical social, cultural, economic, and religious transformation without ever taking the country to war. Nor did he have to face down an uprising. This is extraordinary when one recalls the wars and murderous repression that swept so much of the Arab world during the three decades of his rule.

Tunisia's pioneering role in women's affairs was achieved with the support of Tahar Haddad, a modernizing Tunisian Islamic reformer who called for freeing women from all of their bonds. A scholar of Tunisia's Great Mosque of the Zaitouna, he wrote a hugely influential book entitled *Our Women in the Sharia and Society* (1930), in which he advocated formal education for women and maintained that Islam "had been distorted and misinterpreted to such an extent that women no longer were aware of their duties in life and the legitimate advantages they could expect."[26] In the name of Islam, Haddad denounced abuses against women such as repudiation, whereby a husband could divorce his wife without grounds or explanation, sending her back to her family or leaving her for another wife.[27]

Consider in this context the issue of the veil, an obsession of Islamists everywhere for whom such pious trivia always outweighs genuinely important issues such as unemployment, poverty, and corruption. The veil was seen by Bourguiba as a form of control, both of men and women, in that it inherently postulated that women are weaker, need to be protected, cannot be trusted, are possessions of men. The veil was banned in all Tunisian government buildings and state-funded institutions, and Bourguiba himself denounced it as an "odious rag." Women were discouraged from wearing the veil in the street, precisely because it created a sense of division and inequality between the sexes. For the Tunisian state, the veil and *niqab* symbolized women's oppression, deriving as they do from a backward form of Islam practiced by the Bedouin tribes of the Persian Gulf—a form of Islam rooted, not in the religion itself, but in premodern tribal mores. Mosques were shuttered outside of prayer time, and the call to prayer itself was banned outside the historic old quarters of the country's cities.

Group prayers were likewise discouraged. If you want to pray, the idea was, then you are free to do so; but as an individual, not as part of a group led by an imam who knows nothing but Wahhabi dogma and has taken it upon himself to promote what in his blinkered view he sees as virtue and to condemn what he sees as vice. Tunisians had even grown up with the idea that fasting during Ramadan, compulsory in much of the rest of the Islamic world, was perhaps better avoided. Bourguiba once took a sip of orange juice live on television during the fasting hours to emphasize that fasting made workers less productive. What the country needed was a workforce totally committed to building its modern future.

All this explains why the overwhelming majority of secular-minded middle-class Tunisians—who, according to the World

Bank, constituted some 80 percent of the population at the time of the revolution (measured by home ownership, schooling levels, and income)[28]—did not take to the streets during the uprising. The biggest demonstration is thought to have numbered just 50,000. It also explains why they so quickly lost all patience with the small groups of activists who continued to demonstrate during the months after the regime fell.

TOWARD THE END OF HIS RULE, Bourguiba began showing signs of senility. In November 1987, his former head of public security and then prime minister, Zine El-Abidine Ben Ali, staged a bloodless coup. He did so with the help of the Italian military secret service SISMI. The immediate trigger for this quiet, cloak-and-dagger business had been Bourguiba's threat to execute a group of the Islamists he so despised. It was a decision so out of keeping with his decades-long benevolent rule that it alone was considered by regime insiders sufficient proof that in his old age he had lost his mind. The decision also caused a great deal of outrage in neighboring countries. The Italians, in particular, feared that it could destabilize the entire region—and, with it, an oil pipeline they had built through Tunisia. Neighboring Algeria was already in the midst of a bloody Islamist-inspired civil war that would claim the lives of more than 150,000 civilians. Libya, Tunisia's other neighbor, was routinely accused of sponsoring terrorism far beyond its shores.

However, this was long before the September 11 attacks. At the time, the killing of Islamists—even those convicted of carrying out lethal attacks—was considered "too energetic," as the head of SISMI put it,[29] rather than, as it would later become, a welcome demonstration of where a Middle Eastern country stood in the war on terror. So quiet was the Tunisian coup against Bourguiba, indeed, that a commentator later described the transition as "remarkably unremarkable." Unlike most putschists in the history of the world, Ben Ali was smart enough to honor his hugely popular predecessor in a great many ways. The uprising saw Ben Ali's portrait being torn down by irate crowds throughout the land, but the main streets of almost every Tunisian city are still called Avenue Bourguiba—and there are no plans afoot to change that reality.

During his years in the secret service, Ben Ali had formed close ties with the Italians and the U.S. Central Intelligence Agency (CIA). Although the CIA had no hand in the coup, it smiled on it indulgently. Ironically, Ben Ali, too, was later to present himself to the Americans as a bulwark against the rising Islamist threat. After September 11, he became one of the Bush administration's most trusted allies in the region. Initially, though, his own dealings with the Islamists were relatively benign by regional standards. He either threw them in jail for a while and quietly released them later, torturing some in the process, or he ordered them into exile (which usually meant London). It is worth emphasizing again that not a single one was executed or fell victim to "targeted killings" by the security forces. That has been their fate at the hands of more brutal regimes like Saudi Arabia (and less brutal ones like America). Soon after taking office, Ben Ali released the imprisoned founder of the main Islamist group Ennahda ("Awakening"), Rachid Ghannouchi. But he had him rearrested when Ghannouchi went straight back to promoting Islamism.

In the West, and for good reason, Ben Ali was seen as a "soft" dictator, along the lines of Lee Kuan Yew of Singapore or Park Chung-hee of South Korea. He restricted political freedoms for the sake of stability and economic development. He was a guarantor of stability. *Tunis wa aman!* was the regime's slogan: "A safe Tunis!" For decades it was repeated like a mantra by the masses. Ben Ali's regime, moreover, was not randomly brutal as was, say, Egypt's. Western newspapers reported that a policewoman slapped a vegetable seller, causing him to take his own life and spark the revolution, yet it never happened.[30]

The regime drew clear red lines: Do not call for an Islamist or a Communist state, or a rapid move to democracy. It persecuted, through the extensive network of secret police, those who crossed those red lines. But in their dealings with ordinary Tunisians, the regular cops were as polite and respectful as anywhere in the West—with exceptions that exist everywhere. And there was recourse to the law.

In 2007 I decamped to Tunisia to write my book on Egypt. At that time I would often meet up for coffee with a university student studying philosophy. One evening he was late, even by Arab standards of punctuality. When he arrived he looked shaken. A friend of his, who worked as a doorman at a local nightclub, had been set upon by two drunken off-duty cops, he told me. The fight culminated in one of them headbutting his friend, which left him concussed and with a broken nose. My friend was late because he had been looking after his friend and sorting out the paperwork to make an official police complaint. As it happens, I was in the middle of writing a chapter on torture in Egypt at the time. I could not help but marvel at the idea of two cops being brought to justice in an Arab country. In Egypt such random acts of brutality were the norm. Even doctors refused to give medical certificates to the victims, for fear of being beaten up by plainclothes officers. However, my Tunisian friend was adamant. "This isn't Egypt," he told me. He said the two cops had already been arrested, and his friend would press charges.

During much of Ben Ali's rule, Tunisia was meanwhile nothing if not an economic success story. The reforms he spearheaded, including privatization and opening of the country to foreign investment, bore ample fruit. During his first twenty years in office, the economy grew on average 5 percent a year. Per capita GDP more than tripled, from $1,201 in 1986 to $3,786 in 2008.[31] The Davos Economic Forum Global Competitiveness Report ranked Tunisia first in Africa as recently as the 2010. Tunisia is a country with hardly any natural resources and a large agricultural base. But Ben Ali, as already noted, reduced the poverty rate to less than 4 percent, among the lowest in the world. He continued his predecessor's championing of gender equality and free education and health care for all. And he kept his nose out of ordinary Tunisians' private lives. He pursued a moderate, pro-Western foreign policy, seeking to mediate between Israel and the Palestinians and trying to temper the views of Yasser Arafat's Palestine Liberation Organization (PLO). Tunisia had played host to the PLO from 1982 until 1993 after it was routed from Lebanon during the civil war.

On the other hand—and it is a big other hand—Ben Ali gradually established a personality cult of his own. It is entirely conceivable that he would have been reelected even with a free and fair vote. Instead, it was always with an implausible 90 percent. And he twice changed the constitution to enable himself to become president again. He stared out at his people from the front page of every newspaper every day. Posters of his increasingly waxy-looking visage adorned rather too many large surfaces in cities and villages. The older he got, the more facilities he named after himself. Yet he was by no means a tyrant. Nor did he head a tyrannical regime. Despite the sometimes ugly form his repression of political freedoms took, Tunisia remained an extraordinarily beautiful, pleasant country. It had none of the suffocating atmosphere of Saudi Arabia, the windswept megalomania of the old Soviet bloc, the bland tedium of Singapore. Public services hummed along in a way that put many Western countries to shame. The people were urbane, tolerant, charming, and well educated. They usually spoke excellent French as well as Tunisian Arabic. There was a thriving artistic and literary scene.

Some, especially the young, chafed at the limits Ben Ali imposed on their political expression, but the vast middle class mostly accepted the payoff. So long as they left certain topics alone, they could pretty much do as they pleased in their own private lives. They kept themselves busy doing what really mattered: making money and educating their children, who grew up in streets so safe they could play outside in the early hours of the morning.

IF THE ECONOMIC PICTURE WAS AS ROSY as I paint it, what brought the Tunisian masses out onto the streets? In short: WikiLeaks and a weakening economy.

The regime was a victim of the arrogance that grew out of its successes. In Tunisia, unlike other Arab countries, the educated citizens expected the well-oiled bureaucracy that ran the country to live up to its historically high standards. When the global economic crisis struck in 2008, Tunisia was not spared. This occurred when, in a country of just 10 million, the number of highly qualified university graduates seeking jobs grew to 40,000 a year. The official unemployment rate was 14 percent. That was not high by contemporary European or American standards. But among recent Tunisian graduates the rate was three times as high. Then came a WikiLeaks cable that detailed extensive corruption among the president's extended family. The ruling elite had grown greedy, corrupt, and arrogant, just as the strong economic growth on which the loyalty of the masses depended became unsustainable. The historic Tunisian social contract, by which the loyalty of the people was bought rather than earned, became untenable.

It was not, though, primarily a question of a lack of democracy that caused the revolution. It was more one of contempt for the way Ben Ali was abusing and squandering Bourguiba's legacy, which was not democratic but had the people's best interests at heart. The middle class could look the other way. They still got a decent slice of the pie. What the regime had not anticipated was the boiling anger among the growing numbers of the young who were disproportionately unemployed. I, too, had been caught off guard. I was certain a revolution would happen in Egypt. But I had taken as just more grumbling the stories Tunisian friends told in the lead-up to the revolution of seething anger among the graduates. I recognized that such fury existed. But I could never have imagined it was so widespread as to culminate in a popular revolt.

Many highly educated but unemployed young people started questioning the political censorship that had existed in Tunisia under Ben Ali. Even YouTube was permanently blocked. It was also natural that a generation who had been told to make certain sacrifices for the sake of nation building should ask themselves when that nation would at long last be done being built. Then the global financial crisis struck. Tourists from hard-hit European countries stayed away in significant numbers. This decline affected not only poor people who made an informal living on the edges of the industry, from selling donkey rides to trinkets, but also relatively well-to-do shopkeepers who depended on foreign visitors. Foreign investment started to shrink. There were ever more smart young people with something to be angry about. An opinion poll carried out during the two years immediately before the revolution showed substantial falls in the number of Tunisians who felt the economy was going in the right direction.[32] The revolution was at heart, then, a revolt against the country's deteriorating economic situation among certain sections of the population, not a general yearning for greater democracy and freedom of expression. In postrevolutionary Tunisia, I have asked dozens of young men and women if the revolt would have happened if their standard of living had been maintained and jobs had been guaranteed for university graduates. Without exception, they responded with a resounding no. As we saw in the introduction, during the initial voter registration drive in postrevolutionary Tunisia, only 16 percent of people bothered to sign up. That hardly suggests a deep thirst for representative government.

Ben Ali could probably have weathered the economic crisis. This was a man who had been universally praised in the West for the deftness with which he handled the transition to a modern economy. The problem with the Singapore model of governance—restricting political freedoms for security and the greater economic good—is that it only works if the ruling elite, and above all the man at the helm, leads by example, avoiding the temptations offered by high office and near-total control of the political apparatus. Bourguiba, as any Tunisian will proudly tell you, died in a modest home and without a cent in the bank. That is why he is still so loved by the masses. What the revolutionary minority in Tunisia could not forgive Ben Ali for was personal.

IN 1992, BEN ALI, then in his forties, had married a woman named Leila Trabelsi, who is often described as a "hairdresser." One of eleven children of a fruit-and-nut seller in the old market of Tunis, she came endowed with all the go-getting instincts and blind reverence for family ties such backgrounds always entail. Before Ben Ali's first marriage was dissolved, Trabelsi had borne him a child. As soon as she was safely installed in the presidential palace, five years later, she embarked on the monumental task of turning the whole country into a version of what she knew best: the bazaar.

Her battalion of low-life brothers and an army of extended relatives got their fingers into more and more pies. Ben Ali himself came from a so-called old family and had been nurtured by Bourguiba. His betrayal of Bourguiba's legacy meant his own immediate relatives grew so appalled by the antics of his wife and her tribe that they had publicly distanced themselves from him.[33] The Trabelsis, in contrast, were very much new money. They seemed hell-bent on proving every prejudice the world harbors against such people. From my reading of the situation, they were greedy. They were vulgar. And they did not know when to stop. The American ambassador, Robert Godec, was later to write of the frequent "barbs about their lack of education, low social status, and conspicuous consumption" he heard in his conversations with Tunisians.[34] Leila often sported the large round sunglasses associated with Jacqueline Kennedy Onassis, another woman who owed in part her prominence to strategic marriages to powerful men. But as her cheeks filled out, her eyes vanished in folds of fat, her Chanel suits bulged, her makeup thickened, and her hair hardened into improbable sculptural arrangements, she increasingly came to resemble that archetypal tin-pot dictator's wife: Imelda Marcos. Except that Mrs. Marcos, with her shoes and her jewels and her comically deranged monologues, was by comparison a little pussycat.

To say that Leila was loathed by the Tunisian masses is an understatement. Yet perhaps even the element of snobbery in the universal hatred with which she was regarded by the Tunisian middle class testifies to how well Bourguiba (and Ben Ali in his early years in office) had provided for them. So instead of cheering the rise to the top of a Woman of the People—which is how Mrs. Marcos and Evita Peron endeared themselves to the people their husbands oppressed—they regarded her as a blot on the image of a modern, sophisticated nation they aspired to achieve. At the same time, we should remember—as we descend into the murky underworld of corruption and nepotism created by this odious woman—that while her behavior was nauseating, the consequences were not blatantly obvious for the average middle-class Tunisian. In the same way, the trillion-dollar, tax-funded bailouts for Wall Street bankers, the growing gap between the rich and poor, and the corporate-funded national political system and mass media annoy many middle-class Americans, but for the majority they do not provoke revolutionary thoughts. It took three years for the Occupy Wall Street movement to get up and running. The difference between America and Tunisia, of course, is that America has the safety valve of a democratic system and constitutionally protected freedom of speech. In Tunisia, the anger of the unemployed young had plenty of palpable cause, but no outlet through peaceful, civil society. Marrying his awful wife had been the first step on the road to Ben Ali's ruin. His stupidity in failing to open up the political process and increase civil liberties was the last.

The Trabelsis—their name indicates that they were originally from the Libyan capital, Tripoli, salt in the wounds for the average Libyan-hating Tunisian—were to become known simply as "the Family." They seem to have reveled in the overtones of a mafia clan that term evoked. It was said that in order to get any top job in the country, you needed connections in the Family. It was said that the Family was in the habit of making members of the business elite offers they could not refuse. Whatever they wanted, they simply took. In 2008, one businessman was forced to sell his 3 percent stake in Tunisia's largest bank to one of Ben Ali's relatives at a knockdown price. "A request amounted to an order," he later explained.[35] The Family owned banks, telecom firms, real-estate companies, and car dealerships. So vast was their network of business interests that, when officials sought to untangle it after the Family had left, they decided to leave some of the firms in the Family's hands under a public administrator rather than close them down. Otherwise, some sectors of Tunisia's economy might have collapsed.[36]

The Family kept growing. Their spawn in turn got married, like was drawn to like, and they displayed an uncanny knack for picking the worst of the worst for a spouse. One of Ben Ali's sons-in-law was Sakher El-Materi, the son of a general. He kept a pet tiger that ate four chickens a day at his ritzy villa. Materi junior was widely reported to have deftly profited from Ben Ali's economic policies by investing in and reselling companies that were being privatized. In 2006, he reportedly bought a 41 percent stake in the Tunisian subsidiary of the Swiss food giant Nestlé from state-controlled Banque Nationale Agricole for 3.6 million Tunisian dinars (about $2.6 million today). Nestlé now claims it did not get a say in the deal. Without wishing to impugn the name of a helpless global conglomerate, it is worth recalling that, in similar situations, such firms have been happy to ensure that they have the best possible connections with the ruling families in countries where that is a business consideration. Be that as it may, it has been reported that a mere eighteen months later, Materi sold his

Nestlé-Tunisie stake to the parent company for 35 million dinars, a profit of nearly 1,000 percent.[37] Nice work, as they say, if you can get it. And in Tunisia, unless you were a member of the Family, you increasingly could not.

A better example still of the mafia methods the Family employed is Imed Trabelsi, another of Leila Ben Ali's relatives. It is alleged that he simply shook businesses down by way of a bogus charity for which his goons would come round collecting cash. He also had legitimate companies, but they specialized in things like razing historical areas to build shopping malls. His favorite line was said to come from the movie *The Godfather, Part III*: "Never hate your enemies. It affects your judgment." His own judgment, however, was plenty affected. He finally made it onto Interpol's most-wanted list when he stole a yacht. Unfortunately for him, the fifty-four-foot boat did not belong to an unconnected Tunisian, who would probably have had to write off the loss, but to a Frenchman who headed an investment bank. Having some connections of his own, the Frenchman insisted on getting it back. France, a long-term backer of Ben Ali, made some noise and demanded Imed's extradition. The boat was quietly returned, according to a witness, "in perfect shape."[38] French prosecutors promptly dropped the charges, perhaps instructed to let a small wrong pass for the sake of a greater good. French government ministers, after all, had been on the Ben Ali gravy train. When their free holidays and similar sweeteners came to light following the Tunisian revolution, a number had to resign.[39] Still, at least one Tunisian in the end proved less forgiving. If the uprising was relatively bloodless in light of what was to come elsewhere in the region, at least Imed Trabelsi, who, as admirers of the mob like to put it, "lived by his own code," died by it, too. On January 14, 2011, he was stabbed to death at Zine El-Abidine Ben Ali International Airport, Tunis.[40]

As security guards looked indulgently on, Tunisians looted, pilfered, smashed glass and mirrors, and urinated into the Family's lavish seaside villas. They recalled in great detail every iniquity perpetrated by these lowlife thugs: their vicious dogs that terrorized neighbors' children, their vulgar ostentatious parties. "No, no to the Trabelsis who looted the budget!" was one of the more popular slogans of the uprising.[41] The final insult, many believed, was that Leila was said to have flown to Saudi Arabia with more than $50 million in gold bars from the national bank. There is no evidence proving the truth of that accusation, and it seems improbable. But the Tunisian underclass felt there was a ring of truth to it. And her doting husband did not help whatever case he may have had when he relayed through his lawyer the story that he had meant to return to Tunisia the moment he had safely deposited his wife in Saudi Arabia, but that the pilot ("disobeying orders") took off without him.[42] If you put your wife ahead of your country, and cannot even get the pilot of your own plane to wait for you, what use are you anymore to anyone?

What did the protestors want? They wanted what they had, only better: more jobs and opportunities unobstructed by the Family. Sadly, all indications are that that is not what they will be getting. In June 2011 in a trial lasting all of six hours, a kangaroo court convicted Ben Ali and his wife, in absentia, of theft and unlawful possession of large sums of foreign currency, jewelry, archaeological artifacts, drugs, and weapons—these last "found" in their home weeks after they had been deposed. This suggests that the rule of law was not among the immediate gains of the revolution. "It is a big disappointment, the kind of charade of summary justice that the dictatorship had accustomed us to," the France-based Tunisian rights activist Mouhieddine Cherbib said ruefully. "We wanted a real trial, a fair one . . . a trial of the dictatorship with people who were tortured appearing as witnesses—a justice system from which you learn something."[43]

SOON AFTER BEN ALI'S OUSTER, opinion polls began to report that the largest single party to benefit from the ensuing chaos would be a group calling itself Ennahda. Figures like 25 percent, 30 percent, and even 35 percent support were being bandied about. But the harder observers looked, the more difficult they were finding it to establish what or who Ennahda were. Only two things were certain: that Ennahda had an Islamist agenda, and that it had played no obvious part in the protests that led to the regime's collapse. Its leaders had been in exile or prison. Its grassroots were said to lie in the dusty rural hinterland and working-class suburbs. When extremist violence flared up in the wake of the revolution, moreover, Ennahda denied it had anything to do with it.[44] When a new constitution was being debated, Ennahda insisted on being included in the body that was to write it, but when asked what the constitution ought to contain, its leaders appeared to have no opinion. Wherever observers looked, they found Ennahda an undeniable presence and, at the same time, a baffling absence. It was there and not there. Then how was its popularity to be explained? And what would Ennahda do with the parliamentary heft that it seemed likely to win?

Rachid Ghannouchi, the leader of Ennahda, who has consistently denounced terrorism and violence, embodies its mystery to such an extent that he could almost be seen as being not a real person at all but a strange, newly minted creature, risen from the wreckage of history like Godzilla from the slime. The official account goes as follows.[45] Ghannouchi was born in 1941, the youngest of ten siblings, in Al-Hamma, a village near the southern industrial city of Gabes without electricity or running water and with a single steam-powered radio. His father Muhammad, a farmer, had earned himself the title of sheikh by being the only villager to have memorized the Quran: and so, under his tutelage, did little Rachid. Ghannouchi was later to recall the harmony that prevailed in the family between his father's four wives, of whom he remembered his oldest stepmother with particular affection. An uncle was an ardent admirer of Gamal Abdul Nasser and communicated his love of pan-Arabism to his nephew. Young Rachid also witnessed the emergence of armed resistance against French colonialism and conceived what he later called "an unlimited hatred" of the French colonizers.[46] At the age of thirteen, he was taken out of school, partly to work in the fields, but also because his father objected to the French curriculum, which he felt undermined the purely Islamic education he wished his offspring to enjoy.

However, an older brother became a judge in the city of Gabes and sent enough money home to allow Rachid to resume his education at a school affiliated with the main mosque in Tunis, Zaitouna.

Two years later, his aging father moved the entire family to Gabes, where Ghannouchi later claimed he was first exposed to the effects of modernization. Brothels! Bars! Indifference to prayer! Ghannouchi later parlayed the culture shock the country boy understandably suffered in the port city into the formative experience of his youth. At the time, however, he was sufficiently impressed to read a lot of European novels, study philosophy, and, according to his hagiographer, "even felt he was an atheist."[47] He completed high school at Zaitouna University in Tunis, where, clever student that he was, he had been the bane of his teachers. His ambition first became evident when, after a couple of years as a primary-school teacher, he decided to go to Cairo University, where he enrolled in an agriculture course. A committed Nasserist, he nonetheless disliked the Nasserist reality—it might be said of Ghannouchi, as of many an idealist, that he never saw a new environment he liked—and in any case he promptly fell victim to the expulsion of Tunisians by Nasser due to a disagreement with Bourguiba. Instead, we next find him studying philosophy again in Damascus, Syria. There his political interests diversified, and he joined a host of pan-this or pan-that parties, from the Party of European Socialism, an international forum of Social Democrats, to the Socialist Union, a Nasserist outfit. However, he also regularly went to a mosque run by the Muslim Brotherhood. In 1965, he set out to spend seven months working and traveling in Europe, where he again claimed to be mightily shocked by the goings-on among the "lost and decadent youth" of the countries he visited.[48]

So back to Damascus he went, there to experience his own Damascene moment. For after all these years on first-name terms with philosophy, he later claimed, he suddenly discovered the obvious fact that the pan-Arabist movement had its roots in un-Arabic thought and, indeed, owed much to European socialist internationalism. Disgusted, he turned away. "For I was, and still am, convinced that Islam is the spirit of this Ummah, its maker and the builder of its glory, and is still its only hope for victory and progress," he later wrote.[49] Inevitably, he found the answer among the ideologues of the Muslim Brotherhood, whom he encountered in various mosques around Damascus. Reading the account, you come away feeling that he must have been to these fundamentalist haunts what the drunk is to seedy bars, first one in in the morning and last one out at closing time. And behold, on the night of June 15, 1966:

> I embraced what I believed was the original Islam, Islam as revealed and not as shaped or distorted by history and tradition. That was the night I was overwhelmed by an immense surge of faith, love and admiration for this religion to which I pledged my life. On that night I was reborn, my heart was filled with the light of God, and my mind with the determination to review and reflect all that which I had previously conceived.[50]

And that, as they say, was that.

Ghannouchi nonetheless set out for Paris, because only an education there, his friends told him, would provide him with the needed legitimacy in the eyes of his countrymen. He immediately fell in with a group of Catholic students, presumably because any piety was better than none. After a year of this terrible "test" he had had enough, and so it was that, when he returned to Tunisia, he joined others of his kind in setting up a group devoted to social reform based on Islamic principles that was later to become Ennahda.

HOW MUCH THIS TALE OWES TO REALITY, and how much to the nineteenth-century bildungsroman young Rachid supposedly devoured on a hillock overlooking Gabes, is in a way beside the point. What emerges is not so much a plausible biography but a sort of hagiography: an idyllic childhood in a primitive Muslim community, liberally peppered with quaint anecdotes about goats, loving wives, and lovable pan-Arabist uncles, before the pious youth is uprooted and thrown into the steaming cauldron of modernity whence, after a period of confusion and quest, he returns to the values of his childhood, only purified, strengthened, matured, and with a sharper eye for the dangers it faces and the adaptations it needs to make to reassert itself in a corrupt age.

To begin with, Ghannouchi kept a lowish profile at home and concentrated on the Salafist, Islamic, and Pan-Arabist International—with which he had apparently not broken as decisively as he later made out. He did a great deal of listening to a fundamentalist preacher in neighboring Algeria, but at the same time, splitting hairs in the laborious way of the Islamic scholar, he kept an eye on the international situation. He expressed views, as I understand, not many of them helpful, on the extent to which the Palestinians ought to compromise with the state of Israel. And as late as 1990, he was to hail the staunchly secular Baathist

Saddam Hussein's invasion of Kuwait as uniting at least two Arab countries that the Western colonizers had, in his view, split asunder.[51]

It seems to be a trope in the biographies of great Muslim thinkers that they use the time in prison to reflect deeply and internalize their religion. However, Ghannouchi also used the time to reconcile his deep-seated revulsion to all things modern and his intellectual love of modernization, between his backwater patriotism and his dutiful adherence to the greater Islamic community, between his urge to dictate and his idealization of "the people." Over the decades, he has therefore concocted a strange amalgam of Islamic fundamentalism, Tunisian nationalism, and sentimental socialism, to which, as far as I understand it, he still adheres. But this "journey to democracy" he had his hagiographer describe *always* ends in the same cul-de-sac:

> The Islamic state's function is to accomplish Islam's objective of creating a "community" that dedicates itself [to] the establishment of good and justice and for combating evil and oppression. For fourteen centuries, Islam's relationship with the state was never severed. . . . It was the Western colonizers who used force to replace Sharia law by Western law in the Lausanne Treaty. This was only possible with the collaboration of an elite, including people like Bourguiba and Ataturk, that viewed Islam just as a secular Christian would his religion, considering it an obstacle that hinders progress and development.[52]

He is for democracy "as a system of government and a method of change"[53] but—and here comes the conversation stopper—only insofar as it is compatible with Islam. The Quran remains the sole authoritative basis for legislation, whose earthly manifestation are the scholars (scholars like Ghannouchi) who interpret it so that the state's function is essentially executive in nature. To put it in a nutshell: Islam is the answer to everything, the final authority, and the sole source of legitimacy of government.

AFTER SOME YEARS AS A HIGH-SCHOOL philosophy teacher and a flurry of international activity, Ghannouchi emerged more prominently on the Tunisian political scene in 1981, when Bourguiba relaxed restrictions on political activity and he founded a party he called Ittijah Al-Islami, or the Islamic Tendency Movement. Whether that was merely a clumsy name, or whether it was an early example of Ghannouchi refusing to nail his colors too visibly to the mast, is unclear. The Tendency's ostensible aims, at any rate, sounded even more moderate: the "reconstruction of economic life on a more equitable basis, the end of single-party politics, and the acceptance of political pluralism and democracy"[54]—except that this list must be understood in light of what we have seen he means by "democracy," about which more follows.

By then, though, any mention of Islam was a red rag to Bourguiba. In July the same year, Ghannouchi was arrested, tortured, and given his eleven-year jail sentence. The arrest sparked widespread protests from both religious and secular groups, and in 1984 Ghannouchi was released and resumed his political activity. This was to become the pattern throughout his political life. No matter how moderate his expressed aims, he never once let up for a second. That suggests he was fired up by overweening ambition, in which case he has played a very long game indeed. Or else by a profound conviction whose nature he has been careful to fudge but for which he was prepared to endure almost any amount of suffering.

After several releases and rearrests, in 1992 Ghannouchi went into exile in London and was not seen again in Tunisia until the Ben Ali regime had been ousted, by which time he was in his seventies. Yet news of his imminent return sent women from urban professional and bohemian backgrounds out into the streets, because they believed they had much to fear from him.[55] Ghannouchi denied this was so: "Why are these women afraid of me?" he demanded. Pressed, inevitably, about the headscarf, he added: "Why don't 'liberated' women defend the right of other women to wear what they want?"[56] The matter is always trivial for the Islamist until he is in a position to defend and enforce it, and then it suddenly becomes very important indeed. In my view these women's concerns were right and can be seen from Ghannouchi's peculiar rewriting of feminist history in the Arab world:

> For women, there was no path to freedom, knowledge or self-determination except through a revolt against Islam and its mores and the imitation of the West—until the Islamist movement. Before the emergence of the Islamist movement, woman found herself in an unstable and decaying society whose "liberation" was purely superficial: nudity, eroticism, leaving the house and the intermingling of the sexes.[57]

Given his fundamentalist credentials, parallels were drawn to the return to Iran from exile of the Ayatollah Khomeini. Khomeini had hijacked an uprising by a motley pro-democracy coalition with which he had little to do and, in the end, turned Iran into one of the worst and most repressive Islamist regimes the region had yet seen. Ghannouchi was equally quick to deny the parallel. "Why do people want to compare me to [Osama] Bin Laden or Khomeini, when I am closer to Erdogan?" he has asked.[58]

The reference is to Recep Tayyip Erdogan, prime minister of Turkey. His Justice and Development Party (AKP) has pursued a program of creeping Islamization from the bottom up and from the hinterland in, along with organized harassment of secular intellectuals and artists and gradual erosion of the secular credentials of the Turkish state through the legislative enactments. It has increased Islamic schools and sacked university presidents it deemed too secular.[59] Like Ghannouchi, the AKP has often denied this agenda, while smartly buttressing the enterprise with frantic economic modernization—Islam, after all, is the most friendly among major religions to personal property and a fan of privatization (which is not at all Communist). The AKP has turned Istanbul into one of the most expensive megacities in the world, and it has given rise to rhapsodies in the Western press to the "Anatolian entrepreneur,"[60] a figure whose untrammeled greed is only matched by his superficial reactionary piety. That is the face of moderate Islamism in action. It is worth listening to Ghannouchi expand on the subject:

Since you mention Turkey, most of my books and my articles have been translated to Turkish, and form part of the reference point for the AKP.

The Turkish experience remains the closest to the Tunisian situation, culturally, politically and socially, Turkey is the closest case to Tunisia. So Ennahda, if you were to compare it, cannot be compared to the Taliban or Iran, the closest comparison would be to the AKP.[61]

He influenced *it,* we notice, not the other way round. But Ennahda has no ostensible economic program or indeed any practical political program of any sort (although, as Ghannouchi has assured a questioner, no fewer than 150 university professors are "working on it"[62]). Then how is Tunisia to be governed?

We do not want power to be monopolized by any single party no matter who it is. We want a system that is based on coalitions because only this will protect us from tyranny. We seek a state in which the executive, legislative, and judicial powers are separate, the rule of law is supreme, and the freedoms of conscience, expression, and association are guaranteed.[63]

Of all Ghannouchi's lofty statements of principle, this quotation is by far the clearest. It is also, on my reading, the most chilling. What I believe he is doing is offering the liberals a power-sharing deal: We will let you handle matters such as energy policy and taxation, on which, frankly, we have no opinion, and in turn you will let us pursue our social agenda of Islamizing Tunisian society from below.

ENNAHDA WAS EXTRAORDINARILY EFFECTIVE in accomplishing its immediate political aims by muscling in on the Political Reform

Committee, the most important of several bodies formed to deal with the democratic transition,[64] and lobbying (albeit unsuccessfully) that the interim government be purged of all remnants of the old regime. Its great advantage is that, having been victimized under Bourguiba and Ben Ali, its own charge sheet is clean. The party has taken full advantage of this, with constant commemorations of its "martyrs" held in town squares up and down the country. Ghannouchi himself is mobbed at huge rallies like a rock star. Observers have come back from Tunisia again and again impressed by Ghannouchi's leadership and by how highly organized and well funded Ennahda is.[65] Ennahda has organized mass weddings and picked up the cost, opened countless offices where political agitation is combined with charity work, been seen hanging outside of school gates offering refreshments and candy to the kids studying there, and distributed fliers offering free private instruction to high-school students to help them pass their examinations.[66]

At the same time, no one has been able to pin down what Ennahda is organized *for* and of what exactly Ghannouchi's remarkable leadership consists. Ask Ghannouchi, and he says he just wants everything to stay the same. "We will not try to change the code in any way," he has said of the Personal Status Code introduced in 1956 that protects women's rights. "We see it as compatible with Islamic law. The code was written in the 1950s by Tunisian Muslim scholars . . . through *ijtihad* or the reinterpretation of holy texts. . . . It will be respected."[67] In other words, Tunisia already is an Islamic democracy, so what are you worried about? Islamic law? "That is not among our demands."[68] Yet across the country, people are describing how highly organized gangs of thugs come round, remove the imam of their mosque, and install an extremist preacher without consulting the locals.[69] Secularists, artists, and unveiled women are being attacked by highly organized thugs everywhere in the nation. The brothels and bars that so shocked young Rachid when he first came to the Big City are being torched left, right, and center. While there is no evidence that Ghannouchi and Ennahda were responsible, ask Ghannouchi, and he is the Man Who Wasn't There:

> *We have seen some people preaching on Avenue Habib Bourghiba. In the name of your movement, could you just explain who these people are and what they're preaching about?*
> I have not heard about them.

> *So you do not think that there's a grassroots movement growing in Tunisia, trying to gain support for your movement? It's nothing that you have, perhaps, instigated?*
> There are many that have grown up while we were absent, we have been forced to be absent from the scene for thirty years . . . and generations have grown up and been influenced by our thoughts. Many have, for example, set up Facebook groups in our name, but officially they are not members.[70]

Even so, this undisputed leader of a highly organized movement has no ambitions for high office. "I am not going to run for president of Tunisia, nor as a minister nor as a parliamentarian," he has said.[71] Can we even be sure we know what he looks like? On panel discussions at international conferences, he wears spectacles, a gray suit, and an open-neck shirt, every inch the respected dissident academic. When preaching, he wears flowing robes and a traditional Tunisian cap, every inch the sheikh. The same clipped beard does service for both.

There have been attempts to equate moderate Islamist groups with the Christian Democrats of Europe, as though Christianity did not have a 600-year head start on Islam as far as secularization goes, quite apart from the far less hands-on nature of the mainstream European churches in the present day. From my understanding, the closest parallel, in their odd combination of highly organized structure and denial of responsibility, is with the European far right and the Christian fundamentalists of the United States. Neither has viable views on day-to-day policy. And both could be said, in indirect but important ways, to rely on a grassroots network of thugs whose activities they publicly disclaim. The Bible Belt vigilantes are regularly disowned by the Republican far right, which is nonetheless widely understood to be wooing their vote as if its life depended on it. More specifically, Ennahda, for its part, faces the complication that there exists in Tunisia a movement of even harder-line Salafis: angry young men who want an Islamic state right here, right now. Could it afford to alienate what will be a sizable part of its electoral support?

This, it seems to me, is the explanation of the Tunisian mystery: Ennahda essentially relies on a kind of double consciousness, whereby nobody knows, yet everybody knows, what it is, and where it wants to take Tunisia: away from Paris and toward Mecca. When it comes to eradicating Tunisia's liberalism, the political Islamists and the street thugs disagree on tactics, but ultimately see eye to eye. "Some of the oldest democracies, such as Britain and France, had ministries for the colonies," Ghannouchi has written. "The same democracies, in which homosexuality, fornication, gambling, abortion, and birth control have been legalized, impose unfair conditions on weaker nations."[72] Britain, it should be pointed out, may well be one such cesspool, but it readily offered this man a refuge from political persecution in London for two decades. "Brothels, taverns, gambling houses, usurious transactions, and displays of dance and nudity are all licensed by the authorities and protected by law," Ghannouchi has nonetheless complained.[73] Ghannouchi is not a liberal or moderate in any meaningful sense of either word as I understand them. Bourguiba was, and that is why Ghannouchi obsessively criticizes the legacy of Bourguiba's secularism. And it is precisely his litany of horrors that, for the past half century, made Tunisia unique in the Islamic world.

After the revolution, when asked what Ennahda thought of alcohol, he was ever the diplomat. "We do not like it," he said. "But we do not deal with people by forcing them to do things, but by convincing them."[74] On the question of whether someone who wants to enjoy a beer can drink it, the only truly moderate stand for Ghannouchi—or anyone else—would be, not to seek to "convince" the other not to, but to mind his own business. More tellingly, Ennahda's sleek propaganda on this issue, as on so many others, was betrayed by a lower-ranking member, who stated that banning alcohol could not in fact be ruled out as one of the group's long-term aims.[75] So much for Ghannouchi's earlier quoted comment that "the rule of law is supreme, and the freedoms of conscience, expression, and association are guaranteed." In the short term, perhaps. And always provided they do not bulge, or threaten to bulge, or threaten to lead to behavior that bulges, out of the straitjacket of whatever he thinks of as Islam.

Ask Ghannouchi anything about freedom of expression and behavior, and there is always the massive qualifier of the committed Islamist. Here is his appalling response to the attacks on secular artists in the wake of the revolution. "Art is linked to the values and traditions of each society, and no one should take away freedom of expression through art, *as long as it reflects those traditions* [my emphasis]."[76] The brothels have already been closed. How long before abortion is prohibited and polygamy is again legalized? Before gays start to be rounded up? Before the "odious rag" becomes mandatory for workers in public institutions, and then for women who visit them, and then everywhere?

ETTADHAMEN, THE WORKING-CLASS SUBURB OF TUNIS, was the center of revolutionary unrest in the country's capital. Despite the relentless efforts of the regime over the decades, Islamist currents had always remained strong there. After the revolution, the suburb descended into chaos and was periodically rocked by violent rioting and looting. Ennahda quickly moved to fill the vacuum and deployed volunteers to restore order. Their presence was welcomed, for obvious reasons. As one resident put it: "Tunisia is crashing into a wall."[77] Ettadhamen is a microcosm of what lies in store for the whole country.

Lesser-known liberal political parties have formed a coalition to try to stop the Islamists in their tracks, but the Islamists are winning the war on the ground, and the momentum is on their side. They also have the trump card of never having to prove in practice the validity of their argument. If things do not work out as they promise, they have a get-out clause: The people have not yet embraced Islam with the requisite fervor. Radical Islamists will seek to eradicate the country's secular inheritance by dragging Tunisia, chanting and ululating, back to the Middle Ages. They will be helped by the absence of a unifying structure and the rule of law. The Islamists are ready to prey on society's victims and disadvantaged by intimidation and promises of rewards in the afterlife. To be sure, burning brothels or vandalizing synagogues will not balance the budget, but it will continue to help release frustration. And if a man without any power at all is suddenly given a little power—such as the power to harass women he considers insufficiently shrouded—history shows that he can turn into a very dangerous creature in a very short period of time.

By October 2011, it had become crystal clear whose agenda would ultimately triumph. That month, a crowd of Salafis stormed a university in Sousse and threatened a professor with machetes and sticks after university officials had refused entry to a female student wearing the niqab. A week later, a television station was attacked after it aired an animated film deemed blasphemous by the zealots. The station's director offered a frank apology; but that did not stop a mob of hundreds from burning down his house, forcing his wife and children to flee for their lives through a back entrance.[78] The following Friday, tens of thousands of radical Islamists poured onto the streets of the capital and other major cities, after being whipped into a frenzy by prayer leaders.[79] It was the biggest demonstration since the ousting of Ben Ali, and the chants by the swarms of bearded men waving flags and banners with Islamist slogans were for the creation of an Islamic state. It seems clear to me that the fate of this once beautiful, Islamist-free country was then sealed. Tunisia's unique secular inheritance was fundamentally undermined by the Jasmine Revolution, which from a secularist's point of view was perhaps the dumbest and most self-defeating uprising in history. In October 2011, when Tunisia's first post-revolutionary national elections took place, the pattern I am highlighting in this book—of Islamists gaining a majority of seats from a minority of total support among the population—was confirmed. Ennahda dominated a Consultative Assembly after gaining a plurality of 41 percent of the votes cast. The turnout was 80 percent; but not, as was deceptively reported by the Western media, 80 percent of the total Tunisian population, but rather 80 percent of the 50 percent who had bothered to register to vote. In other words: Ennahda won despite the fact that more than 80 percent of all voting-age Tunisians did not actually vote for the party.

TWO

EGYPT'S ISLAMIST FUTURE

I ARRIVED IN LUXOR, EGYPT'S MAIN TOURIST TOWN IN THE SOUTH of the country, in May 2011. Three months earlier one of the most popular revolutions in history had culminated in the resignation of the country's reviled dictator, Hosni Mubarak, after three decades of his increasingly brutal and chaotic rule. Since my first visit to Luxor in the early 1990s, I have dreaded each return trip, which I nevertheless make once or twice a year in order to visit a wonderful family I had befriended.

The city's attraction is the pharaonic sites, which can be seen in a day or two, and that is how long most foreigners stay before they are flown to Cairo on the next leg of their carefully choreographed group tour. For travelers who know the grim reality hidden in the shadows of the monuments, the city makes for a depressing experience. Government neglect and endemic poverty means that, aside from the constant hassle tourists must suffer from the legion of touts, many of the city's young men become prostitutes as the only hope of earning a living. In the 1990s, Luxor became the center of male prostitution in the Middle East. The studs sold themselves to older foreigners (the john's gender made no difference), who arrived throughout the year for unabashed, but for the most part locally denied, sex tourism.[1] Luxor's mayor, Samir Farag, was arrested after Mubarak's ouster on charges of rampant corruption, as were many other mayors up and down the country; but a few years earlier he had told an Arabic-language newspaper that as many as 30 percent of Luxor's young men had married an older foreign woman, and in most cases this was covert prostitution[2]—the latter being both illegal and shameful for the conservative locals to openly acknowledge. I was loath to return to Luxor because even if as a single Westerner you are not on the lookout for street meat, you are still solicited by the city's rent boys and pestered for cash by the tourist hustlers. Not, of course, that the two groups are mutually exclusive.

Now, for the first time in almost two decades, I was looking forward to my Luxor sojourn. Surely, I told myself, the city could not be in worse shape than the capital, Cairo, my home for most of the previous decade, the biggest city in Africa where some 20 million mostly impoverished individuals struggle to eke out a living. During Mubarak's tenure it seemed miraculous that Cairo's inhabitants managed to survive from one day to the next. The traffic congestion, compounded by the blatant refusal of drivers to follow even basic rules of the road, meant that traveling from one district to another could take up the best part of a day. The pollution left anyone wearing white regretting the decision the moment he stepped onto the street. And the city was so densely populated that, over the years, I had increasingly found myself taking a stroll during the middle of the night, the only time it was possible to have a moment's peace. Still, the city had been secure enough to allow anyone to do just that. One could indeed walk anywhere at any time without fear of falling victim to even petty, opportunistic crime.

After the revolution, however, the police retreated from the streets. Crime rates, in addition to even more insane driving, predictably soared—partly as a result of mass jailbreaks during the uprising and partly as a deliberate policy on the part of the regime in its dying days to foment chaos as a way of warning of the power vacuum that would come with its demise. The police themselves had their own disruptive agenda. They had been attacked by revolutionaries because of their well-earned reputation for beating and torturing suspects. Now they refused to leave their stations, even when serious crimes were reported, in order to teach the Egyptian people a stark lesson in the wisdom of bowing down to authority.[3]

Because for a while I had lived in Shubra, a vast working-class district in the north of Cairo, I was eager to pay a visit to my old neighbors there to ask about their experience of the revolution. I arrived late in the afternoon, and the conversation soon turned to how it would be best for me to leave before dark. Nobody, they said, ventured out after the sun went down. In the old days, at least one family would have offered to put me up for the night. They were too polite to admit it, but I think the rank xenophobia encouraged by the new interim military regime, and stoked by the Islamists, as a way of deflecting attention from pressing but irresolvable social and economic problems, meant they no longer wished to be associated with a foreigner—even one who was quite well known in the neighborhood for having written a critical book on the Mubarak regime. Vigilante squads were in the habit of "arresting" any foreigner they came across and then turning them over to the military so the evildoer could be investigated as a potential spy.[4] Other cities in Egypt suffered crime, too. In postrevolutionary Alexandria, the country's second city, located on the Mediterranean coast, the security situation was even more dire than in Cairo. So frequent had kidnappings become as a way of extorting money from wealthier families that locals were taking their children to school in convoys guarded by armed parents, and men openly carried guns to protect themselves from muggers.[5] In Suez, the main city on the Suez Canal, armed robbery, rape, and murder had become so common that nipping round the corner to stock up on necessities was a risky undertaking, especially if it meant leaving a family of only females in the house alone.[6]

As the family in Luxor had reassured me in advance, the revolution had left the tourist city in a much happier state. This was paradoxical, in that some 90 percent of the locals depend on a tourist trade that had come to a sudden halt. I was often the only foreigner in the hot, dusty streets I wandered through, but the locals found sweet compensation for the lack of customers: even fewer police were at their posts. Here the police had been especially cruel and arbitrary in their dealings with the residents as a way of ensuring security for the millions of tourists passing through. During the revolution, all the police stations were attacked by armed local tribesmen. Most were then burned to the ground.

As elsewhere in Upper Egypt, and in contrast to the bigger cities, the tribal aspect of the local culture had resulted in life quickly returning to normal in Luxor—or, as I was repeatedly told, rather better than what had previously passed for normal. In quiet, traditional tribal communities, reputation matters above all else. The importance of maintaining individual and family honor meant few in Upper Egypt had taken advantage of the chaos for personal gain; and there were no deep-seated tribal rivalries or territorial disputes that threatened to break out into civil war.

Egyptians are among the most patriotic people in the world: they are Egyptians first and foremost, and their profound sense of national pride ultimately trumps their often strong tribal allegiances. And they were united by a single, common goal: the removal of Mubarak. Above all, there was a huge sense of relief in Luxor that being in the wrong place at the wrong time would no longer result in a volley of kicks and slaps or worse, delivered by some bored, underpaid officer acting with impunity.

The main fear throughout Upper Egypt was that escaped prisoners were stealing livestock. At night men with hunting rifles took turns sitting watch, shooting into the air whenever a barking dog warned of the presence of strangers. In Luxor even the petty hustlers had largely disappeared. I assumed this was because, since there were no tourists to harangue, leaving the house was not worth their while; but an old friend offered what struck me as an equally valid explanation. The touts, he said, had always blamed the Mubarak regime for their woes and reprehensible behavior: If the government is so shameless in robbing the country blind, who can blame us for fighting among ourselves for the crumbs that fall from the table? Now that the regime had been overthrown, they were more inclined to take responsibility for their actions. Bad behavior, he suggested, was an insult to the revolution's ideals. The tourist center of the city was small enough for everyone to know everyone else, so it was possible for a sense of collective goodwill to take hold in a way that clearly was not the case in the huge metropolises like Cairo and Alexandria.

There was a second reason I had decided to make the trip, in addition to visiting the local family. Back in downtown Cairo, I bumped into a friend from the Christian Coptic minority, who make up between 10 and 15 percent of the Egyptian population. They had mostly dreaded a revolution because they feared it would bring the fundamentalist Muslim Brotherhood to power, who would then push to turn Egypt into an Islamist state. Egyptians are very big on greetings, and even if they saw you only yesterday they are likely to ask about your health, family, and work as though you had not chatted for an eternity. But my Coptic friend, although it had been a few years since we had met up, dispensed with those formalities. Instead, when he saw me in a downtown street he broke into an ironic chant in mockery of the revolutionary slogans that had filled Tahrir Square calling for the country's liberation from tyranny and repression:

Hurriya! Hurriya!
Salafiya! Salafiya!

Freedom! Freedom!
Salafism! Salafism!

Salafism is a catchall term used to describe extremist Islamists who shun modernity and believe in returning to the simplicity of life as experienced in the early days of Islam, or as it is thought to have been experienced. There is little practical difference between the beliefs of the Salafis and those of the Wahhabis of Saudi Arabia, and their adherents are easily spotted in that they tend to wear flowing white robes and sport long beards. Although Wahhabism had made deep inroads in Egypt (as elsewhere in the region) since the 1970s, the idea of a sectarian Salafist doctrine had remained alien to most of the population. The Muslim Brotherhood, the most popular Islamist group in Egypt, had worked hard to promote a relatively more moderate agenda that embraced, superficially at least, both modernity and democracy. And the Mubarak regime had tirelessly battled more radical Islamist groups, who had launched an insurrection against the state in the 1970s that culminated in the 1997 massacre of dozens of tourists in Luxor.

After the fall of Mubarak, Salafist groups had been sprouting throughout Egypt. Nobody knew where they came from. But they were blamed for a string of deadly attacks on Copts and their churches, as well as against the shrines of Sufi Muslims—the latter number in the millions and are considered by the Salafis infidels because they worship local saints.[7] Salafis hijacked mass demonstrations against a newly appointed Coptic governor in the southern city of Qena, soon swelling the numbers from a few thousand to tens of thousands. Many waved the Saudi flag.[8] And in July 2011, they descended on Tahrir Square in the hundreds of thousands in the biggest demonstration since the revolution and demanded that Egypt be declared an Islamist state with strict, Saudi-style religious laws.[9] That broke a postrevolutionary pact with the liberal, leftist, and secular groups that had led the uprising.

By this time, revolutionary fervor among the general population had waned. The pro-democracy activists' calls for continued mass demonstrations, in protest at what had effectively been a military coup resulting in the army taking over the day-to-day running of the country, usually attracted just a few thousand demonstrators. As in Tunisia, these demonstrators still blocking streets in protest at the refusal of the old guard to give up power now had to face not only the riot police but irate locals, too, who attacked them with equal passion.[10] For most Egyptians, the revolution had achieved its goal by ousting Mubarak, and they wanted life to return to normal under the auspices of the hugely popular military council, whose generals had opted to force Mubarak to step down rather than fire on the Egyptian people to keep him in power. In the minds of the Egyptian masses, a famously patient people, the memory of the revolution was so fresh that they could still hope that it would usher in a brighter, more prosperous, and freer future. Eight months after Mubarak's ouster, in October 2011, an opinion poll found that 90 percent of Egyptians still had faith in the country's new military rulers, despite the fact that they had reneged on an initial promise to hand power back to civilian rule with six months of their having seized it.[11]

That the Islamists were taking the initiative in the chaos of post-Mubarak Egypt came as no surprise to my Coptic friend. For years, terrified at the prospect of an Islamist takeover in Egypt, he had applied annually for a visa to emigrate to America. Like me, he had long since been certain that a major upheaval was on the horizon and that the consequences would be catastrophic for the country's liberals and religious minorities. As we chatted, he mentioned that Al-Gamaa Al-Islamiya, the Islamist terror outfit responsible for the massacre of dozens of tourists in Luxor in 1997, was planning on holding a huge rally—in the very same city where the massacre took place. This encapsulated for him how all his fears were becoming reality with terrifying rapidity.

When I reached Luxor a week or so later, there was indeed talk of little else. The group's members, who formerly had been hunted down by Mubarak's security forces, announced the imminent gathering by driving through the streets with huge speakers strapped to the top of their cars and throwing fliers advertising it out of the windows. One afternoon I was in a coffee shop when a group drove by. A boy waiter picked up a flier and held it above his head, declaring in a loud voice that someone at last was telling the truth. The guy sitting next to me derisively whispered in my ear: "That donkey can't even read and write."

All the better for the Islamists, I suggested. In a conservative country where as many as half of the population may in fact be illiterate, and where there is a deep historical apathy when it comes to the nitty-gritty of political debate, empty religious slogans coupled with bold reassurances about how the truth will set you free have much more sway. And if, I told my companion, the radicals are finding a constituency in this city—perhaps the most liberal and welcoming of foreigners in the country, and completely dependent on being so for its economic survival—it was hardly surprising that they were making such dramatic inroads elsewhere.

On the day of the rally I made my way to Luxor's main square. Thousands of bearded, white-robed Islamists had gathered to listen to a series of lectures given by the Al-Gamaa Al-Islamiya's leadership. A few soldiers sat on a nearby wall chain-smoking. Otherwise there was no security: this for an open gathering by a group still designated as a terror outfit by America and the European Union. However, it turned out to be a publicity stunt, held in front of Luxor Temple to dispel the notion that the group was pagan-hating fanatics. Still, in September 2011, the group's application to register as a political party in order to compete in upcoming elections was rejected by the interim military council, despite their having already granted such licenses to the Muslim Brotherhood (under a new name: the Peace and Justice Party) and to a slightly less extreme group of Salafis calling their party El-Nour (The Light).[12] The military, justifying the group's continuing ban on the grounds that the constitution forbids explicitly religious parties, had reason to be skeptical: The evening following the official lecture in Luxor, an even greater crowd gathered at the same spot to witness the conversion of a local Coptic Christian to Islam. Word in the souk was that the man was insane and had been promised a house, wife, and job by the Salafis for embracing the True Religion. The ugly event exposed the hypocrisy of the talk on the previous evening, in which Salafis had applauded as Copts were welcomed in speech after speech as fellow Egyptians with equal rights and a minority whose religion should be respected. In October 2011, Al-Gamaa Al-Islamiya, whose leadership of course was nowhere to be seen on the night of the conversion, won an appeal in Egypt's high court against their application to register as a political party.[13]

The fact that only a few thousand Islamists had attended both meetings, out of a Luxor population of some half million, might offer cause for hope that their pulling power was limited— although, looking at it another way, that so many could flock to listen to the leaders of a group that had committed such a ghastly terror attack so recently and just a few miles away was deeply alarming.

More cause for hope might be had in a national Egyptian holiday called Sham El-Naseem, when Muslims and Christians alike celebrate the arrival of spring by indulging in the pagan ritual of a predawn swim in the Nile followed by a picnic. As always, a week or so after the Salafi gatherings in Luxor, all but the die-hard fanatics joined in the festivities. This is the kind of convergence of events that allows liberals to argue that the Islamists are a minority, and Egypt's long tradition of pluralism, tolerance, and diversity, not to mention its intriguing mishmash of Islamic, Christian, and pagan traditions, will ultimately face down the threat of an essentially alien dogmatic Islamist ideology.

It is perfectly true that the Islamists are the minority; but so, to emphasize it again, were the followers of Ayatollah Khomeini during Iran's 1979 revolution. To this day, the majority of Iranians, too, continue to celebrate their own pre-Islamic festival, called Nowruz, despite the best efforts of the mullahs to put an end to it. Iran has protected Jewish, Christian, and other minorities, who were publicly embraced by Khomeini when he returned to the homeland. Nevertheless, the Iranians have been living under the rule of an extremist Islamist regime for three decades and counting.

There is no contradiction at all, then, between a largely non-Islamist population being ruled over by a hardline Islamist minority. The Islamists just have to be better organized. And in that regard, when revolution broke out, Egypt was far more ripe for an Islamist takeover than was Iran in the 1970s.

IN EGYPT, UNLIKE IN TUNISIA, almost all the people supported the revolution. Having spent a decade in the country, talking with the sort of Egyptians you never see in a glossy holiday brochure, I knew well the hardships that large swaths of the population had struggled with. A husband could be holding down two jobs and still bring in less than $60 a month. A wife could struggle to put meat on the table more than once a month. Her children could pass all their exams with flying colors and still be illiterate, for in Mubarak's Egypt it was not hard work that brought exam success. So widespread was the corruption, and so chronically underfunded was the education system, that a pass rate was obtained with a packet of Marlboro Lights and a few dollars slipped under the table by a parent too weary—or too frightened—to buck the corrupt system.

Among ordinary Egyptians, fear and pent-up anger had become almost default states. Mubarak's police force had become infamous for its mass roundups, random arrests, and savage beatings, regardless of guilt or innocence. Each gross injustice provided another recruit to the opposition cause—and after thirty years of Mubarak's brutal regime that was an awful lot of recruits. In one village, a boy of thirteen was arrested on suspicion of stealing a packet of tea. He was beaten, raped, and left for dead on wasteland for his parents to find him.[14] That entire village wanted revenge. Similar stories were repeated all over the country.

There was another crucial difference between the Tunisian and Egyptian revolutions. In Tunisia the army had played no part in politics, but in Egypt the military establishment had been the real power behind the presidency since the 1952 coup that overthrew the British-backed monarchy and brought to power Gamal Abdul Nasser and his so-called Free Officers. Every Egyptian president—Mohammed Naguib, Nasser, Anwar Al-Sadat, and Mubarak—has been a military man, and it was often said that while the president governed, the military ruled.

In Tunisia, when Ben Ali fled, the power vacuum was filled by the old civilian guard, but it so lacked authority and popularity that enough space was left for other, competing political parties and voices to emerge. In Egypt, however, it was the military that forced out Mubarak, and then a small number of generals appointed themselves as interim rulers. In other words, there had been a military coup. Egypt moved from being a military dictatorship with a military man acting as president to being a military dictatorship.

Initially, both the masses who had poured out onto the streets and the small number of pro-democracy political activists whose initial acts of brave defiance had inspired them were content with this outcome. The revolution's sole goal was the removal of Mubarak. But accustomed to power, wealth, and influence, the country's military elite saw no reason why that should change. That view was undoubtedly shared by those demonstrators who called for democratic reforms for almost three weeks—a fact that might surprise those in the West who consider a military coup to be little better than the military-backed dictatorship it replaced. But the fact is the army is not unpopular in Egypt. Its soldiers did not turn on the demonstrators, and, in a country where every adult male has to do military service, that sense of "them and us" does not exist. This is the same army, after all, that intervened and organized a massive increase in bread production in 2008 when major cities were threatened by shortages and long queues developed outside every bakery. The truth is that the soldiers are very much ordinary Egyptians. Thus the new regime was given some flexibility in how—and when—long-awaited reforms were delivered.

However, it quickly became clear that the generals were more interested in consolidating their power than furthering the goals of the revolution. In the months following Mubarak's resignation, more people were summarily tried in military courts under the country's emergency law than had been tried during the whole of Mubarak's three decades in power.[15] The generals summoned journalists for interrogation whenever they wrote anything deemed too challenging to the new regime and were accused by human rights groups of routinely torturing detainees.[16] As of September 2011, only one police officer had been charged with murder when more than a thousand protestors died during the uprising. Most of the ministers appointed to a transitional government had previously held ministerial positions in the Mubarak regime. Mubarak and his hated sons, Gamal and Alaa, were put on trial, but after months of delays, and the trial itself turned out to be farcical, with dozens of lawyers often punching and kicking each other and a constant retraction of key testimony by witnesses.[17] In September

2011, a leading Egyptian human rights organization declared that human rights abuses in the country were now worse than they had been under Mubarak.[18]

None of this should have come as a surprise. The military had had three decades to rein in Mubarak and his thugs, but had done nothing. Their hijacking of the revolution was actually a repeat of the events that brought them to power in 1952. In January of that year, massive anti-British riots left half of Cairo in smoldering ruins; it was a mass uprising that held all the promise of bringing about genuine and radical change in the country as it emerged from colonial rule. But the following July, Nasser took advantage of the unrest to launch his coup, then set about eradicating what freedoms had existed for the previous half century by banning opposition parties, canceling parliamentary elections, nationalizing and censoring the press, and outlawing labor strikes.

In 2011 the pro-democracy activists had from the outset foolishly declared their own revolution "leaderless"; they had learned nothing from history about how revolutionary movements lacking a vanguard are crushed by more entrenched and better-organized forces in the aftermath of massive social and political upheaval. But they had no constituency to speak of anyway. I quoted in the introduction a poll among those who demonstrated in Tahrir Square that showed only 19 percent of them had been motivated by a thirst for freedom and elections.

A few weeks after Mubarak was deposed, a small women's rights group held a demonstration in Tahrir Square to mark International Women's Day. The organizers had called for a million-woman march to ensure the revolutionaries put female emancipation at the heart of their reform agenda. A few dozen turned out. Even they were not safe from the Tahrir mob, who screamed insults at them, sexually assaulted them, and told them their proper place was in the home washing dishes and taking care of their children.[19] Other female demonstrators were reportedly sexually assaulted and tortured after they were arrested by the military, with a number even given "virginity tests" to prove that they were promiscuous and therefore completely beyond the pale for most Egyptians.[20] What was even more shocking than these incidents was that, at a time when demonstrations were breaking out everywhere on a whole range of issues, not a single man came to the women's aid when they were being assaulted in Tahrir or protested their sickening treatment at the hands of the military. Shocked feminist activists, usually from the English-speaking elite, were then given to telling the international media with a heavy sigh that a revolution that failed to advance the rights and needs of half the population was no revolution at all. And they were right. Nor could it by any stretch of the imagination be described as liberal and freedom-loving.

IF FAILING TO ORGANIZE POLITICALLY was the pro-democracy activists' main failing during the revolution, putting their trust in the Islamists after Mubarak left office was an even bigger one. It again showed how they knew nothing of history, and in particular the Iranian Revolution, in which the liberals had likewise formed an alliance with the Islamists, only afterward to be slaughtered by them. The Muslim Brotherhood had refused to back the revolution, partly because it has always been a conservative movement against radical and sudden change but also because its leadership must have feared massive repression in the form of arrests and torture if it did join the demonstrations. But the social decay during Mubarak's three decades in power in Egypt had strongly increased the Islamists' appeal—which Mubarak in turn exaggerated to keep Washington's calls for reform to a whisper. The Muslim Brotherhood was formed as a fundamentalist group in 1928 with the aim of Islamizing Egyptian society from below, and thus purging the country of decadent Western influence and customs. During Nasser's years in power the group was persecuted, and most of its members fled to exile in Saudi Arabia, where they became immersed in the even more extremist Wahhabi ideology. In the 1970s, Anwar Al-Sadat invited them back and used them to counter the leftists who had emerged as a powerful opposition force in the country. It was at this time, at the height of the oil boom, that millions of Egyptians traveled to Saudi Arabia and other conservative Persian Gulf countries to work. They, too, grew accustomed to Wahhabi customs, which they would bring back with them—making them a natural support base for the newly empowered Muslim Brotherhood.

Mubarak should at least be given credit for his deft exploitation of Washington's fears about the Muslim Brotherhood after he took power in 1981, following Al-Sadat's assassination by Islamist extremists enraged that he had signed a peace treaty with Israel. It's either the Muslim Brotherhood or me: that was Mubarak's mantra. There is no evidence that the Muslim Brotherhood has in fact ever been able to count on the support of more than a minority. And for that reason the Muslim Brotherhood used Mubarak's persecution of its rank-and-file members with equal shrewdness: to elevate its status within Egypt and, perhaps more important, among the champions of so-called moderate Islam in the West. Before the revolution, it had ratcheted up some resounding successes in Islamizing Egyptian society from below. A month before Mubarak's downfall, a poll conducted by the Pew Research Center revealed that a majority of Egyptians support stoning as a punishment for adultery, hand amputation for theft, and death for those who convert from Islam to another religion.[21]

Sensing its moment was nigh, the Muslim Brotherhood—harboring a long-cherished goal of establishing an Islamist state—dramatically increased its sway in the postrevolutionary land of the pharaohs. When Youssef El-Qaradawi, the fundamentalist group's spiritual guide made famous by his weekly television show on Al-Jazeera, visited Cairo, he was able to deliver a political sermon to as many as 5 million of the Egyptian faithful in Tahrir Square.[22] Those in the West who interpreted the Islamists' lack of presence on the streets during the uprisings as the birth of a pluralistic Egypt were, it now became crystal clear, very wide of the mark. Revolutionary upheaval was always going to benefit the Islamists. And for all that their media-savvy spokesmen—and they are always men—pay lip service to democracy and pluralism, the Islamists are guided by the belief that a return to the fundamentals of Islam is the solution to everything. They want to Islamize their societies, either from the bottom up or, if given the opportunity and at a time when they are absolutely certain of attaining power, from the top down.

Egypt is now a deeply conservative country that, over the past two decades, has so pervasively succumbed to the Wahhabi customs promoted by the Muslim Brotherhood that, in some cities, you might as well be in Saudi Arabia. After the revolution, a poll in Egypt suddenly reported that 75 percent of the people support the Muslim Brotherhood.[23] That seems an implausible conversion rate from a mere 30 percent before the revolution. But perhaps the experts had been wrong all along? Opinion polls, to be fair, rarely reflect what people really believe, especially in autocratic countries where people have for decades been used to saying one thing in public and thinking another. However, they are excellent at gauging what people think they ought to think. Essentially, they illuminate the moral atmosphere in which people must try to live. As such, the opinion poll was perhaps instructive.

In any event, as a hint of what is now in store for Egypt, consider the city of Alexandria—for decades the Muslim Brotherhood's stronghold. Once it was a cosmopolitan summer resort famous for its secular, carefree atmosphere. Now it is about the least fun place to live in North Africa. All Muslim women in the city are veiled, among the young often for fear of otherwise being labeled whores by the unemployed guardians of public morality; and violence between local Christians and Muslims is commonplace. Extremist Muslims rioted in the city when the postrevolutionary regime happened to appoint a local mayor who was a Christian. Most bars have stopped serving alcohol. The only women to be found on the beaches, even in the height of summer, are those taking care of their kids—and they are invariably covered from head to toe in black. Sadly, Egypt is now so conservative and reactionary, and the progressive elite so out of touch, that the Brotherhood's battle cry—Islam is the solution—drowns out more subtle calls for moderation.

IT WAS ONLY AFTER EGYPT'S DICTATOR had been ousted that the Islamists started infiltrating the demonstrations—and then reportedly under strict orders not to draw attention to their affiliation or alienate delirious Western pundits by mentioning the caliphate or by burning U.S. and Israeli flags.[24] Instead of showing their true colors, they mobilized their youth wing, the Shabab Al-Thawra (Youth of the Revolution), to hijack uprisings that were still being hailed in the Western press as Twitter and Facebook revolutions. At first glance, this may seem baffling. But the Islamists are unique among the world's political parties in that their goal is not to attain power merely for the sake of attaining power. Indeed, what the Islamists prefer is to work with a government that takes all the responsibility for running the country but is sufficiently docile to allow them to impose their cultural tyranny. To succeed, they do not need majority support. All the Islamists require is to be louder, more forceful, and better organized than their opponents. That is another reason why the Muslim Brotherhood, instead of backing the uprising, initially preferred to stick with the extant regime: that way they could have continued the game of doublespeak with Mubarak while busying themselves with their important God-ordained task of imposing their cultural fascism on society. And that is why, after the revolution, they immediately ruled out running for the presidency and announced, moreover, that they would be contesting no more than 50 percent of the seats up for grabs in parliament. With real power comes responsibility and, crucially, accountability, and the Islamist consider themselves accountable only to Allah.

In keeping with its desire to work in opposition while distancing itself from real power, reports soon began to appear that the Muslim Brotherhood had entered into a pact with the military establishment. In return for the group being granted legal status and permission to stand in elections, it would call its members off the streets and lobby instead for continuation of the military-sponsored state.[25] The Islamists have little interest in devising tax or energy policy, about which the Quran is silent. Bereft of sensible, let alone practical, solutions to the real ills that plague their society, they seek cultural influence. The toothless Egyptian parliament has for decades been the Muslim Brotherhood's preferred arena, charitable work among the poor being their chief recruitment tool. Their charitable deeds are now more in demand than ever. The revolution left the Egyptian economy in tatters. For all the optimistic Western comparisons to the collapse of Communism, Egypt is much more like an action replay of Iran in 1979. Like the Egyptians, most Iranians did not want to live in an Islamic theocracy. The Iranian Revolution of 1979 is always described, inaccurately, as an Islamic revolution, but in its initial stages it has a striking similarity to Egypt's in January 2011. The masses on the streets were drawn from all sections of Iranian society: the working class and the middle class, Marxists, anti-imperialists, feminists, right-wing reformers from within the system—and, yes, Islamists, too. In the chaos of postrevolutionary Iran, Khomeini's

Islamist forces emerged as the strongest, most disciplined, and best-organized opposition, and he was most revered and charismatic leader. This is why his Islamist hordes in Iran were ultimately able to triumph, whence they set about slaughtering the rivals who, just months before, had put their trust in them as revolutionary comrades. Regardless of their minority support, the Islamists in Egypt are likewise poised to fill the vacuum. Then they will impose their agenda on the majority, although there is still much cause for hope that this will not happen with the same level of tyrannical violence and brutality as was the case in Iran.

Evidence that the Muslim Brotherhood's softly-softly approach will bring them success abounds. In the midst of the social breakdown of post-Mubarak Egyptian society, for example, Egyptians voted on a redrafted, postrevolutionary constitution. Only 41 percent of the eligible voters bothered to make their way to the polling booths—an astonishingly low turnout for the first free and fair elections most Egyptians had ever had. In the run-up to the referendum, just two political groups had urged a yes vote: former dictator Mubarak's National Democratic Party and the Muslim Brotherhood. And yet more than two-thirds of those who voted heeded their call. Parties representing the secular, progressive Egyptian elite, who had vigorously campaigned against the revised constitution, arguing that they needed more time to organize, were decimated. The Muslim Brotherhood, moreover, won the referendum simply by claiming that any further changes to the constitution would somehow facilitate an American and Israeli plot to delete Article 2, which states that Islam is the official religion.[26]

The pressing question, then, when it comes to Egypt, the most populous Arab country and the region's historic trendsetter, is what kind of society the Muslim Brotherhood wants to create. Of some things we can already be sure: more anti-Western, more Islamic, and fervently anti-Zionist. The Muslim Brotherhood's main foreign policy aim (apart from tearing up the country's peace treaty with Israel and opening up the Rafah border crossing to Gaza) is to reassess Egypt's military and financial dependence on America. Since the army controls the country's foreign policy and is the recipient of the American aid, that will prove a tall order. But in the distant future, they envisage the reestablishment of an Islamic caliphate. Documents published by the group during the last few years make it clear that they believe in Islamic democracy, not the kind that exists in the West. To put it simply: the Muslim Brotherhood will make political participation of individuals in society subject to the principles of Islamic law. In the West, the legislative and judicial branches of government monitor state actions to ensure they conform to democratic rules. The three branches of government keep each other in check. In the Islamist setup that the Muslim Brotherhood (and other Islamist groups throughout the region) aims to establish, actions of the state would be monitored by—well, the Muslim Brotherhood, who would ensure they conform to Islamic law. In other words, the Islamists would monitor themselves.

And what of the idea that the Muslim Brotherhood has mellowed of late? This perhaps has more to do with its recruitment of spokesmen who spout to gullible Western "experts" the virtues of its pro-democracy platform. So effective has their propaganda been that an American official was moved to describe the Brotherhood as "a loose network of secular groups."[27] This kind of ignorance in the West about Egypt presents the Brotherhood with a tremendous opportunity for media manipulation. Scratch the surface, however, and you find a detailed political platform published in 2006. The president cannot be a woman because the post's religious and military duties "conflict with her nature, social and other humanitarian roles." A board of Muslim clerics would oversee the government. The freedom of association guaranteed civil organizations in the West would, in an Islamist Egypt, also be conditional, once again on their adherence to the strictures of Islamic law. Egypt would have a shura (consultative assembly) system, whereby a body of compliant old men nod through whatever the leader, who is assured "veneration," sees fit, while a Supreme Guide presides benevolently over the personal morality of the masses.[28] In Saudi Arabia and Iran, that system exists now.

The Muslim Brotherhood has distanced itself from the attacks on Copts and Sufis but has joined forces to fight elections with the radical Salafi groups. Finding differences between the two groups, aside from the Muslim Brotherhood's clear renunciation of violence, is like splitting hairs. In September 2011 Salafis were calling for the covering of Egypt's pharaonic monuments because they were an affront to its Islamist identity. The Muslim Brotherhood condemned the suggestion, but on the same day launched a campaign to ban the wearing of bikinis on any of the country's beaches because doing so was contrary to its Islamist agenda.[29] The Muslim Brotherhood and various Salafi groups have in fact joined to hold mass rallies and have announced plans to electioneer together.

"The differences between the Salafis and the Muslim Brotherhood are not as significant as some Western experts on Islam have suggested," an academic writing for the Hudson Institute has correctly pointed out. "At the end of the day both parties want to see an Islamic regime in Egypt—one where democracy, moderation, and pragmatism are nonexistent."[30]

In May 2011, a powerful editorial in *The Washington Times* cut through the spin surrounding the Muslim Brotherhood's true aims. It drew attention to an article posted on its website written by Egyptian cleric, Salah Al-Din Sultan. The article, the editorial noted, lauded bin Laden's raising "the banner of jihad for the sake of Allah" as being "in the defense of Islam and the resistance against the occupiers, [even if it was waged] in a way that deviated to some extent from the middle path of moderation." On the other hand, the author wrote, "the terrorism of America is in defense of hegemony, oppression, and tyranny and [aimed at] subjugating the peoples and regimes of the world to American [uni-]polarity." In any case, the author concluded, "bin Laden's terrorism is [merely] alleged, since the accusations against him came from the media rather than from a court, whereas there is no doubt as to the terrorism of America." If these are the moderates, the editorial asked, "imagine the views of the extremists," and it further pointed out that the Obama administration's "critical blind spot in dealing with the Middle East is failing to recognize the threat posed by all forms of Islamic extremism," whether violent or not:

The White House denounces Al-Qaeda's "perverted" views on Islam, yet groups like the Muslim Brotherhood advocate exactly the same thing. Apparently, Mr. Obama doesn't think it's a problem if they achieve Shariah by the ballot instead of the bullet. An electoral victory by the Muslim Brotherhood will herald the death of freedom in Egypt.[31]

THE DANGER POSED BY ISLAMIST TRENDS in Egypt is indeed little understood by Washington, which had propped up Mubarak and his regime just as it once did the shah of Iran—and, as it turned out, with the same outcome. The irony is that the effort to thwart an Islamic revolution in Egypt hastened Washington's own worst-case scenario, and it had devastating consequences for Egypt's historically tolerant and pluralistic culture and, in the long term, for America's influence in the region. Anti-Mubarak anger on the streets of Cairo during the revolution soon became redirected at Washington, Mubarak's paymaster, and Tel Aviv, because of the widespread belief—quite correct, it seems to me—that the administrations in America and Israel were making every effort, to the very end, to keep their stooge Mubarak in power.

Few Egyptians were impressed with Obama's performance during the revolution. Like Mubarak's, Obama's speeches addressed to the Egyptian masses smacked of insincerity and expediency. They were too little, too late, and six months after the revolution his standing in the Middle East was at an all-time low.[32] The countless other human rights violations carried out in the name of the Mubarak regime had largely gone unchallenged by America, Egypt's most important and generous ally in the West, just as Washington has been silent on the sometimes worse violations in the name of the military council since Mubarak's ouster. Valuing stability in the Middle East above all else, and blinded by gratitude for Egypt's signing of the Egypt-Israel peace treaty in 1979, Washington had been pumping money into the Egyptian economy ever since—most recently to the tune of almost $2 billion a year. Most of it goes directly to the military.

The Israelis are used to dealing with the Egyptian military on matters of foreign affairs, so for them the coup underlined a return to business as normal. Indeed, the Israelis did not even have to negotiate through a figurehead president. Instead, they started to deal directly with the same military that has so effectively policed the Egypt-Israel peace treaty for the last thirty years. Washington, too, was clearly relieved at the outcome, happy that the billions of aid paid annually to shore up security in the wider region was money well spent. The military made it clear that the peace treaty with Israel will stand. The fact is that America needs the Egyptian army almost as much as the Egyptian army needs American aid. Small wonder that it is now becoming clear that many of the negotiations during the street protests were not between the White House and Mubarak's presidential palace, but between the White House and Egypt's Ministry of Defense. But there are complications on the horizon. Widespread Arab discontent with America's pro-Israel policy was kept from boiling over by the intervention of strong military rulers such as Mubarak. Now that that level of control is gone, angry and violent anti-American and anti-Israel protests are sweeping the country. In September 2011, a mob torched the Israeli Embassy in Cairo, and its diplomats had to flee under armed escort from Egyptian commandos.

There has been much talk about how Turkey could provide a model for postrevolutionary Egypt; it has a secular and pro-Western military elite keeping in check a strongly emergent and fiercely anti-Western Muslim Brotherhood. But this analogy falls apart on closer inspection. Atatürk, modern Turkey's founding father, was a military man who was staunchly secular, and the constitution he wrote explicitly gave the military powers to defend the secular state against efforts at Islamization. That is why, over the past decade, it is the Islamists in Turkey who have repeatedly been dragged before the courts and charged with violating the state's secular principles. In Egypt since the 1980s, it is liberals who have been dragged before the courts for allegedly blaspheming Islam. Nasser initially formed an alliance with the Muslim Brotherhood to help seize control of Egypt, and Article 2 in the Egyptian constitution clearly states that sharia is the basis for the country's legal system. The truth is that the Egyptian military elite has no guiding political or religious principles. They will accept whatever deal allows them to perpetuate their rule. Living in a kind of parallel world of officers' clubs and gated communities, it matters little to them whether women in the poor districts are veiled or not, whether the bikini is banned on the beaches or not, or whether liberals are allowed to express themselves without the draconian restrictions on freedom of expression the Islamists would dearly like to impose.

America's trump card, of course, will continue to be the aid it pours into Egypt, now needed more than ever. And while Persian Gulf countries are promising much more cash, they cannot offer the military training and equipment Washington provides and without which the Egyptian military would to all intents and purposes cease to exist as a viable fighting force. In the short term, then, Egypt's relations with America and Israel will bumble along as they have for the past three decades. The danger lurks in the longer term. Corruption, poverty, and illiteracy are so widespread in Egypt that it would take a generation under the cleanest government in the world to begin to eradicate them. While the demonstrations have petered out, labor unrest in the country continues. For the Egyptian masses, as we have seen, it is the economy that matters, rather than free and fair elections; and they have proved themselves far from the mass of docile, endlessly patient souls of legend. In short, a new revolution in Egypt cannot be ruled out. If and when it comes, it will aim to overthrow the military establishment. The Islamists will not shy away from it, as happened in 2011. They will lead it.

THREE

THE WAHHABI COUNTERREVOLUTION

AMONG THOSE WHO SUBSCRIBE TO THE KITTEN-LOVING, FACEBOOK Arab Spring narrative, much was made of a sign at the main demonstration in Bahrain's capital, Manama, that read: "No Sunni, no Shia, just Bahraini."[1] It fed perfectly the popular narrative of Arabs hankering for a pluralistic democratic nation-state, all iPhones, smiley logos, and summer-in-the-park. In fact, the Bahraini protests were a Shia uprising against the hated Sunni minority that rules over them with Saudi support and became a sideshow in a bigger sectarian and geopolitical standoff that pits Shia Iran, and the various Shia minorities in the region that gravitate toward Iran, against Sunni Saudi Arabia and its ally America. Only 10 to 15 percent of the Muslim world is Shia, yet they are concentrated in areas that are strategically vital for Iran. Around 85 percent of Iran's population is Shia, as are 60 percent of Sunni-ruled Bahrain. Sunnis make up 85 percent of the Saudi population, but its Shia are the majority in the Eastern

Province, which is home to most of the kingdom's oil reserves. The Iranian regime vociferously backed the Shia uprising in Bahrain in 2011; and, dating back to its 1979 revolution, it has fomented discord among the majority Shia population in eastern Saudi Arabia.

The tiny island of Bahrain is linked by a causeway to Saudi Arabia's Eastern Province, where the Saudi Shia majority have deep grievances against their Sunni overlords. This bridge was built, it is often said, as a way of allowing sex-starved Saudis to find solace in Bahrain's brothels. It certainly serves that function admirably. But there is a reason: the bridge allows Saudi tanks quick and easy access to Bahrain. Since the fall of Saddam Hussein, Bahrain is the only Shia-majority Arab country ruled by a Sunni elite. This makes its elite feel understandably vulnerable and eager to make outside friends—such as the U.S. Navy's Fifth Fleet, which is based there. The fleet has some thirty warships and thousands of personnel and is crucial to Washington's efforts to contain Iran. A successful Shia uprising in Bahrain would have been seriously disruptive to American assets in the Persian Gulf.

And the Saudis, too, were nervous, for good reason. Their archrival is Iran, which has historic claims to Bahrain. Iran has forged links with the 2 million Shia in Saudi Arabia's Eastern Province, who in turn have ties to their Bahraini brethren across the causeway. During the Bahraini protests, Saudi Arabia's Shia demonstrated against the House of Saud in the Eastern Province and in support of the Shia in Bahrain. Iran intervened, warning Riyadh not to crack down and objecting to a Saudi military presence in Bahrain.[2] U.S. Secretary of State Hillary Clinton was by then openly worrying about Tehran forging closer ties with the nascent Shia insurgency in both Bahrain and Saudi Arabia.[3]

For Washington to complain about the interference of others in the internal affairs of Arab countries may well be laughably rich, but that does not mean Clinton's assessment was inaccurate. The mullahs in Tehran, under constant threat of being bombed by Israel because of an alleged clandestine nuclear program, have always regarded Bahrain as the great Shia prize. In particular, the mullahs remember when the Shia in Saudi Arabia's Eastern Province last rose up en masse against the House of Saud: in 1979, in support of Iran's revolution. The bridge to Bahrain was built by the Saudis in the 1980s with all this in mind. After its construction, the Sunni monarchy in Riyadh could rush to defend their Bahraini allies against any Shia uprising and threat of an Iranian takeover. That is what the Saudi military did in February 2011, when the Bahraini protests threatened to gain some real momentum. A thousand Saudi soldiers then took up positions guarding key Bahraini installations as a state of emergency in Bahrain was declared. The Al-Saud ruling family said it would do "whatever is necessary" to prop up Bahrain's Sunnis, and it took just a few days for their tanks to crush the Shia uprising. So far from mirroring the Velvet Revolution, for which Czechoslovakia is now justly celebrated, the Bahraini uprising was an action replay of another poignant moment in that East European country's history: Prague, 1968, when Soviet tanks rolled through the streets and withdrew the country behind the iron curtain for another twenty years.

By exploiting Saudi fear of an encroaching Shia-dominated Iran, the West was continuing a divide-and-rule tactic of its imperial past in the region. In the 1860s, the British had brokered a deal with the Al-Khalifa royal family and installed them as rulers, and they rule Bahrain to this day. Bahrain effectively remained a Sunni-dominated British protectorate until independence in 1971.

One of the most used descriptions of Saudi Arabia is that it is the "home of Islam." Yet the country is a 1930s British geopolitical construct named after a royal family with borders demarcated by the heathen British. The Saudi ruling family conquered a vast area of the Arabian Peninsula in the 1920s with enthusiastic British diplomatic and financial support. Saudi Arabia's first king, Ibn Saud, was on the British payroll, and many of his top advisers were British. And he founded the extremist Wahhabi kingdom in 1932 with full British blessing. For the British, the Wahhabis, although obviously barbarians given to slaughtering everyone (liberal Sunnis, Shia) who were not also committed Wahhabi fanatics and refused to convert, were nevertheless led by a pro-British king. His foot soldiers were the only forces that could tame the vast tribal territory that otherwise would threaten British strategic interests. What goes around certainly comes around in the Middle East, with depressing familiarity.

Meanwhile, the roots of hostility between Sunni and Shia exploited by the West are not found in profound theological differences, but in tribal intrigues that took place in the Muslim world in the seventh century. When the Prophet Mohammed died in A.D. 632, the question of the succession to his leadership was dominated by family rivalries and disputes. There were four candidates to succeed as "caliph," or leader. One group in particular, which went on to form the Shia, strongly favored the claims of Ali, the grandson of Mohammed. The name, Shia, derives from "party of Ali." But three times in succession Ali was passed over, as each of the other candidates was chosen before him. The opposition to Ali deepened the sense of anger among his supporters. Eventually, in this climate of tribal factionalism, Ali became the fourth caliph, though the indignation of his followers was further provoked when he was then brutally assassinated.

The tribal feuding in the post-Mohammed era reached its climax at the Battle of Karbala in A.D. 680. This is the key moment in the creation of the Shia movement, the point at which the fissure was permanently established. In the battle, Ali's son-in-law, Hussein, was killed. The Shia came to regard him as a martyr. The split between the Shia and the opposing faction—which took the name Sunni, or "tradition"—has existed ever since that battle. The division soon acquired the trappings of theology. Fundamentalist Sunnis regard the Shia as heretical because they say the latter's veneration of Ali and Hussein contradicts the Muslim belief that Mohammed was the last Prophet and forbids idolatry. The Shia revere Ali and Hussein, they point out, but do not consider them prophets like they do Mohammed. Nevertheless, the Sunni belief in the heresy and treachery of the Shia leads to repellent prejudice in Saudi Arabia especially, where the Shia are widely loathed. When I lived in Saudi Arabia, Sunnis would often tell me that I should never accept any food from a Shia, because he will spit in it before he hands it over. That kind of routine comment indicates that, although the two sects live alongside one another, it is not an easy coexistence. The Shia in Saudi Arabia face outright discrimination. Partly this hostility stems from the fact that Saudi Sunnis are mainly Wahhabis, a cult that adopts the most literal and narrow brand of Islamic theology. According to the Wahhabi mentality, the act of killing a Shia infidel will improve a Sunni zealot's chance of entering heaven.

The Shia do not regard Sunnis as infidels or heretics. Nor do they feel they have anything spiritually to gain by killing them. This partly explains why nearly all suicide-bomb attacks against Muslims have been perpetrated by Sunnis, and why most suicide attacks in Iraq (often against Shia) were carried out not by Iraqis but by Wahhabi-indoctrinated Saudi nationals.

The moment the Saudi tanks rolled across the causeway linking Saudi Arabia and Bahrain sounded the death knell for the Arab Spring. The invasion served three purposes, in addition to propping up the Wahhabi kingdom's fellow Sunni monarchy in Manama and securing America's crucial navy base. The first was to quell unrest specifically among Saudi Arabia's own newly restive Shia minority in the oil-rich Eastern Province. The second was to prevent Riyadh's archrival, Iran, from gaining greater influence over Bahrain's political process, and by extension among the Saudi Shia next door. The third was to demonstrate that Riyadh would stop at nothing—from soft diplomacy to military engagement—in its determination to lead a region-wide counterrevolution. From the outset, Riyadh had taken a degree of control over the direction of the Arab Spring by offering refuge to Ben Ali, Tunisia's deposed leader. Understandably eager that a precedent in popular justice against an Arab dictator not be set,

Saudi Arabia steadfastly refused to extradite Ben Ali to stand trial. The statements of secular Ben Ali, issued through his lawyer, afterward consistently called on Tunisians to continue the path of modernization. But he was not able, for fear of upsetting his Saudi hosts, to express what must have been his horror at the dramatic emergence of Ennahda, the main Islamist party, onto the Tunisian political scene. Ben Ali had spent decades suppressing Ennahda, and its meteoric rise after he left Tunisia is widely believed to be partly the result of bankrolling by Saudi Arabia and other Persian Gulf states (although concrete proof has thus far not been found).[4]

To tighten its hold on the region, Saudi Arabia promised $4 billion in soft loans and credit lines to bolster the new military regime that came to power in Egypt. And there were also allegations that Saudi money was flowing under the table to help extremist Salafi groups in Egypt.[5] The Saudis were also piling huge pressure on the Egyptian interim regime in the form of indirect threats. These included changing labor laws that could lead to the expulsion of millions of Egyptian workers from the kingdom, a devastating blow, if it happened, to an Egyptian economy already reeling from revolutionary chaos.[6] In Yemen, as we will see below, Riyadh hijacked the uprising through its Islamist and tribal proxies.

At home, the Saudi royal family did what it always does in any crisis, and promised $130 billion in handouts to keep the population in line.[7] Thousands of protestors on Saudi Arabia's own "day of rage"—mostly Shia in the Eastern Province—were quickly dispersed or arrested. The Wahhabi religious establishment then declared religiously forbidden all protests against a regime that already represented God's kingdom on earth.[8] And that was the end of the desert kingdom's Spring. In the years leading up to the uprisings, the "reformist" King Abdullah and his inner circle of smart, smooth-talking, Western-educated hoodlums had become increasingly willing to assert their political weight. The Saudis, astonishingly, sit on the U.N. Commission for Human Rights. And the 2002 Saudi peace plan for Israel and Palestine—two states within the 1967 borders in return for security guarantees from the Arab regimes—forms the backbone of Washington's policy in the region. In Pakistan, the Saudis finance religious education. They fund madrassas around the country from the Pashtun border regions with Afghanistan, throughout the Punjab.[9] In the process, they have inexorably rolled back what little gains that troubled country had made toward a more civil society. In return for massive handouts of oil money, thousands of Pakistani ground troops and mercenaries are reported to be stationed in Saudi Arabia to help the dictatorial royals repress their own people.[10]

In the courts of the West, the Saudis meanwhile launched a campaign to show that, while secular civilian or military regimes may be crumbling, the pious Gulf monarchies are not where this happens. They spread the message that George W. Bush was naïve to think that democracy is the cure of all ills in the Arab world. The example of China and the Asian tiger economies shows that a period of autocratic government is a much sounder guarantor of stable development.[11] And what better proof of their claim than that, in the wake of the uprisings, huge amounts of money flowed from the volatile economies of Egypt and Tunisia to the kingdom, which had more ready cash than it knew what to do with. In turn, Saudi Arabia could conclude more multimillion-dollar arms deals with the United States and Britain and hire more British and American trainers for Abdullah's private army, which was busy shooting unarmed protestors in Bahrain.[12] Take that, democracy!

The Al-Sauds are a pragmatic lot. They can hardly be accused of not knowing what is good for them. They have gladly taken, and paid for, America's security guarantees. In America's wars, they have compromised their fanatical Wahhabi ideology again and again. As I understand the situation, they continue to repress and torture their own people with impunity, while spreading hatred, ignorance, and murderous anti-Western ideology throughout the Muslim and Western worlds. Washington's pragmatic friends, it is clear, are never quite as stupid as the so-called global security experts who influence American foreign policy. The former play the latter like a fiddle. In the wake of the Arab Spring, Obama proved himself the star pupil of his sometime adviser, Henry Kissinger, from whose realpolitik most of the hapless countries that were scorched by it have yet to recover. Obama's bombing of Libya will have consequences as devastating and unforeseeable as the bombing of Cambodia. But there is another close parallel between these two Nobel Peace laureates. Kissinger had a singular talent—some have said a predilection—for choosing the worst possible world leaders to make his deals with, from Suharto of Indonesia to Pinochet of Chile. In our time, what partner could be worse than Saudi Arabia? I would argue that only the Kim Jong-Il regime has a more repugnant record for repression and torture. But at least its influence stops at North Korea's borders. The Saudi royals, though, are still trapped in the deadly domestic embrace with the Wahhabi religious establishment they rule in awkward partnership with. As the British did in the 1920s, America now must politely look the other way as the descendants of the kingdom's founding extremists indoctrinate young men in the Wahhabi-funded schools, madrassas, and mosques of Jakarta and Kabul. Jihadists have swarmed out of the Land of the Two Holy Mosques to wreak havoc wherever the opportunity has presented itself. Saudi Arabia continues to be the principal source of funding for Islamist terrorism around the world.[13]

When King Abdullah, in the halting geriatric mumble that so endears him to a certain kind of Western commentator, announced a package of social handouts in the wake of the Arab Spring to buy off the Saudi population, he also issued a royal decree. It banned the media from publishing anything that "violates sharia," harms "the good reputation and honor" of the senior Wahhabi clerics or government officials, or "damages state interests, serves foreign interests, promotes criminal activity, threatens public order, or harms national security."[14] Given that, despite its rhetoric about promoting human rights and freedom around the world, Washington continues to regard the Al-Saud as a vital guarantor of what policy experts like to call "stability"—shorthand for safeguarding American and Israel strategic interests—the Saudi royal family will be in power for a very long time. There will be no NATO bombing of that country, however violent the repression becomes. In his much-hyped speech calling for democratic reform throughout the Middle East in the wake of the Arab Spring, Obama did his Saudi friends the kindness of not mentioning them, by extension doing all of us the favor of revealing the rank hypocrisy of his lofty democracy rhetoric.[15]

And so all hail the success of America's "engagement" with a Saudi regime that rules over a country where, in the year A.D. 2012, it remains illegal for women to drive a car or leave the house unless accompanied by a male relative, and even then they have to be completely covered in black.

I ONCE GOT LOST IN ASIR, a mountainous, sparsely inhabited region on Saudi Arabia's southern border with Yemen. It was the home of many of the September 11 terrorists, from the local million-strong Al-Ghamdi tribe.[16] Conquered by Saudi forces in the 1920s, Asir was subsequently incorporated into the Saudi state on its founding in 1932. But for centuries until then the region had been fiercely independent. It still retains its distinctive Arabic dialect, traditional local attire, and Yemeni-style architecture. Yemenis and Saudis who live near the border often have dual nationality, in addition to family or tribal links on the other side of it. Not that they need a passport to travel from one country to the other to meet up: Much of the rugged border territory is unguarded and unmarked, and the area's smuggling routes are well established. When I got lost, the most striking thing, to a Westerner used to carefully demarcated and patrolled borders, was that I seemed to be the only person who cared which country I was in. The matter was certainly of pressing importance to me. I had a Saudi residency permit, but not the required visa to enter Yemen. I therefore risked being arrested as an illegal infiltrator if I had strayed into Yemeni territory. After a few hours, I encountered an elderly man with a garland of flowers and herbs in his hair, as is the custom among the males of one of the local tribes colloquially known as the Flower Men. I asked him if I was in Saudi Arabia or Yemen. "It's all the same to us down here," he said dismissively, offering me a drink. In much of the Middle East, the idea of a border police—or for that matter central government—becomes blurrier in this way the farther from the capital one heads. Instead, tribes, more likely to be armed to the teeth than adherents to the cult of flower power, rule their quasi-independent territories like fiefdoms. So while it is natural for the West to think about an integral unit called "Libya" or "Iraq" or "Yemen," very different factors often dominate local actors when there is political unrest or war in the Middle East. Much of the Arab world identifies itself, to put the matter simply, by tribe. If sectarianism was one obstacle to building national unity and progressive policies in the wake of the Arab Spring, tribalism was an even bigger one.

One of the saddest of the many sad stories to have emerged from postrevolutionary Tunisia, the most modern Arab state, where regionalism and tribalism were severely discouraged, was that regional sensitivities and tribal prejudices quickly resurfaced, with deadly consequences. In Metlaoui, a southern mining town, riots erupted a month after the uprising over rumors that a mining company had for some reason decided to recruit employees only from a specific tribe. The result was mayhem: five people were killed and dozens were injured as rival tribal groups firebombed each other's houses and attacked each other with machetes and sticks. The tribal clashes spread to the nearby towns of M'dhilla and Sned. In the historic market of the country's capital, Tunis, local merchants fought with traders recently arrived from the provinces.[17] As these tribal and regional prejudices turned ever more violent, the online Tunisian magazine *Kapitalis* editorialized:

> In the absence of sociopolitical frameworks (a strong government, credible political parties, and representative organizations), people seek refuge in what they consider to be their primary social structures: family, clan, tribe. The sense of national belonging and civic loyalty—if they ever existed in these regions unjustly marginalized and neglected by the state—gives way instead to clan and tribal solidarity.[18]

One can hardly accuse the former Tunisian regime of having "neglected" the capital's historic Medina. Nevertheless, the fact remains that tribalism is as important as Islamism in the region. Both fiercely antidemocratic forces feed off each other. Islamism, I would argue, is like drug addiction, in the sense that it leads only to a craving for even more Islamic Islamism. Its most fertile hunting ground for new addicts is where a brain chemistry of tribalism and its narrow-minded, hate-mongering territoriality exists. Thus the core Islamist supporters in both Tunisia and Egypt are from the countryside, or among families who have migrated from there to the big cities and find themselves adrift in a sea of poverty and hopelessness. If Tunisia, which also has the best-educated population, can revert so quickly to its Islamist and tribal roots (as half of its voting-age population does not even make the effort to put their names on the electoral register), what hope is there for the emergence of representative governments in countries like Libya and Yemen, where tribalism and Islamism have always been, and will remain, fundamental aspects of people's daily lives and belief systems? Their populations are for the most part fiercely anti-American, and decades after independence the remit of the central governments barely extends outside of the countries' capital cities. These two countries were defined by the very absence, to quote the Tunisian magazine *Kapitalis* again, of "a strong government, credible political parties, and representative organizations" *before* the Arab Spring came.

The lessons of the recent past in the Middle East bode ill for the future of Libya and Yemen, the two Arab countries that descended into the bloodiest civil wars. More than a decade after the American invasions of Afghanistan and Iraq, these countries, despite their regular elections, are farther than ever on the social level from Western notions of liberalism and pluralism. The populations in both are busy tearing each other apart along tribal and sectarian lines, while the liberals are so threatened and marginalized they barely manage to get a word in. In Afghanistan, the writ of the corrupt puppet president, Hamid Karzai, still does not run beyond the capital, Kabul. The Taliban, once America's greatest enemy and one of the reasons for the invasion, are looking more and more like an acceptable negotiating partner if the land is to be, if not pacified, then at least becalmed.[19] In Iraq, democratic elections brought extremist religious parties to power. The American-led war allowed Al-Qaeda to get a foothold in the country for the first time. And the coalition was only able to battle jihadists by buying the support of local Sunni tribal leaders. They are never the most open-minded, liberal kind of men one is likely to find in the region. (There is not an abundant supply even in the modern urban centers.) A measure of what a dismal failure this strategy proved is that, as recently as August 2011, Al-Qaeda was able to launch dozens of simultaneous bombings in many Iraqi cities, killing about eighty people and injuring many hundreds more.[20] The same month was the deadliest for American soldiers since the war began almost a decade earlier.[21] Now Yemen and Libya are headed in the same direction as Iraq and Afghanistan.

Yemen, the most tribal country in the Middle East, has spent only two decades as a nominal country, after the north and south were united in 1990. It was torn apart by tribal warfare in the name of the Arab Spring. The fate of its president, Ali Abdullah Saleh, was sealed when the country's vast tribal confederation called the Hashid, from which Saleh himself hails, turned against him.[22] Seriously injured by shelling of his presidential palace, Saleh was whisked off for medical treatment in Saudi Arabia. A subsequent investigation into the attack squarely blamed leaders of his own once loyal clansmen for carrying it out.[23] Given that the country was in total chaos when the investigation was carried out, and its authors had their own agendas to push, it remains anyone's guess how objective the report was. But without the benefit of vast oil reserves and subject to a harsh climate and arid, difficult terrain, impoverished Yemen has always been a hardscrabble, backward, unruly sort of place riven by age-old tribal resentments. An experiment in the imported twentieth-century madness known as Communism naturally was unable to alleviate this situation in the then-independent south of the country. The only way Saleh was able to rule Yemen for three decades was by repression. This had to be done primarily by getting some friendly and important tribes on side to keep down others who were more independent, and therefore a potential threat. The ones who were left out, of course, did not take kindly to the fact. By the time the Arab Spring came to Yemen, it was already breaking apart.

The consequences for the region, and especially for Western interests, of civil war in Yemen are far more serious than the fall-out from Libya. Yemen is of key geopolitical importance. It border one of the world's most strategic shipping lanes, the Strait of Bab Al-Mandib, where the Red Sea meets the Gulf of Aden. This makes Yemen crucial for the safe transport of much of the world's oil supplies. And Yemen's largely impenetrable terrain has for more than a decade proved ungovernable and thereby provided a safe haven, and been the main training base, for one of the most fanatical Islamist terror franchises of them all: Al-Qaeda in the Arabian Peninsula. Saudi Arabia, the world's leading oil producer, especially has reason to be worried about the potential terrorist fallout from unrest in Yemen. Riyadh has long claimed that smugglers from its southern neighbor provide the explosives and weapons used by radical Islamists who carry out attacks in the Wahhabi kingdom. They include two massive suicide bombings of Western civilian targets in 2003 that killed more than fifty and injured hundreds. A former Al-Qaeda leader in Yemen, Saudi-born and educated Mohammed Hamdi Al-Ahdal, revealed under interrogation that both Saudis and Yemenis were involved in funding two major terrorist attacks in Yemen: against the USS *Cole* in October 2000, which killed seventeen American sailors, and against the French supertanker *Limburg* in October 2002.[24]

Saudi Arabia, one of the most vocal critics of Israel's security fence, has even decided to emulate Israel's example by erecting a highly contentious barrier along its porous frontier. It is part of a larger plan to build an electronic surveillance system across the entire length of the kingdom's land and sea borders.[25] This strategy was never likely to succeed. And it is less likely to do so in the wake of the Arab Spring. Yemeni smugglers moving arms and explosives are notorious for developing creative ways to evade Saudi controls. For any crackdown to be effective in stopping the weapons trade, Riyadh relies on the cooperation of a strong Yemeni government. Even when Saleh was firmly at the helm, he never had any direct control over the country's provinces and their tribes. I saw this a few years ago on a trip to Saada, a town on the northern Yemeni border with Saudi Arabia. There I stumbled on an open-air arms market where machine guns, hand grenades, and even surface-to-air missiles were laid out like fruit and vegetables in a Western supermarket. Armed tribesmen had blocked the roads in and out of the city with boulders. Safe passage had to be secured with bribes.[26] Only twenty-five miles from the Saudi border, I was even offered an 85-millimeter surface-to-surface missile—a projectile that could blow through a building—for only $2,500. Antiaircraft missiles, the type of weapon fired at an Israeli jetliner in Kenya in 2003, were no longer on display. But when I asked a few dealers, they told me these heavy weapons were still available for the right price. "There is complete freedom here," a Saada local said proudly. "Anyone can buy whatever they like, as long as they have enough money."

Such arms markets across the country have for decades attracted thousands of buyers each day. There are an estimated 60 million weapons in Yemen: one for every three people. On open display are weapons from China, Russia, Belgium, Spain, and even Israel—a country Yemen does not recognize. During a brief 1994 civil war between the north and south, Saleh paid tribal leaders to ensure their support, which brought him a swift victory. But the tribal leaders in rural areas, whose support Saleh also needed to survive the 2011 uprising against him, had feared that giving up their arms would mean being marginalized from political life. So they refused to close down their weapons souks. Saleh backed down, fearing with good reason a popular uprising: Ibrahim Al-Hamdy, a former Yemeni president, had been assassinated in 1977 in what many believe was a plot by tribal leaders angered by government involvement in their affairs. When the rebellion Saleh had feared finally came in 2011, his tribal enemies were as well armed as his own army.

Saudi Arabia's blatant interference in Yemen's internal affairs after Saleh was bombed out of his palace dramatically increased anti-Saudi sentiment among large sections of the population. Demonstrations often took on anti-Saudi (and anti-American) agendas. This enmity between Saudi Arabia and Yemen will make the arms trade harder to stop. Saudi Arabia has a history of supporting disaffected Yemenis in an effort to manipulate the internal politics of a country it sees as a security threat because of its large population and strategic location. When Yemen was divided into two nations during the cold war, opposition to unification became a stated Saudi foreign policy objective. When Yemen unification took place nonetheless in 1990, the Yemenis routinely accused the Saudis of increasing clandestine funding to various Yemeni insurgent groups. Many tribal leaders in Yemen opposed to the central government in Sanaa remained on the Al-Saud payroll. Yemeni tribes that straddle the border also fiercely oppose its fencing-off. They have attacked workers building demarcation posts and, according to one prominent leader of the Wayilah tribe, have up to 3,000 armed tribesmen who "are ready to fight any time if Saudi Arabia doesn't remove what they have built in our country."[27]

Islamist terrorists represent an even bigger threat than sectarianism and tribalism to Western notions of democracy in Yemen. Al-Qaeda franchises exist in many countries in the Greater Middle East, from Pakistan to Algeria. They benefit from worsening economies and the radicalization of young people—the latter largely thanks to American-led interventionism. Yemen is considered natural territory by Al-Qaeda. It was the ancestral home of its founder, Osama bin Laden, whose death in 2011 in one of those strange, media-orchestrated American raids seems to have done nothing but inspire his followers to carry out more brazen attacks. In Saleh, the country had a leader who was an earnest ally not only of Saudi Arabia but of Washington's war on terror. After he was injured, Al-Qaeda in the Arabian Peninsula became the first group to benefit. In May 2011, hundreds of the group's members descended, under cover of darkness, from the mountains on Zinbijar, the capital of Yemen's southern Abyan province. After a swift raid on a base of the security forces they seized the entire city. The soldiers at the base were no match for them. This was partly because the Yemeni army is chronically underfunded, badly trained, and hopelessly ill-equipped. But it was also because most had already been pulled off to the capital to protect the president. A week later, Al-Qaeda in the Arabian Peninsula seized the city of Azzan, in Shabwa province in the southeast, and announced that it too would be joining the emerging Islamic caliphate.[28] A few months later, Yemeni officials warned that the Islamists were still in control of much of the south of the country and were preparing to implement Taliban-style rule.[29]

This was dismissed as scaremongering by the Yemeni revolutionaries, but that is Al-Qaeda's terrain: soon they were chopping off the hands of petty criminals, including that of a 15-year-old boy who had stolen some electrical cables.[30]

Saleh had initially complained that he had no choice but to go along with America in the wake of the September 11 attacks. But he enthusiastically increased his cooperation with Washington and scored successes with America's assistance. In November 2002, Yemen looked the other way while the CIA used a missile strike from a Predator drone to kill a top leader of Al-Qaeda.[31] The Yemeni government had also rounded up hundreds of Islamist militants. More recent cooperation went even further. The American military were training a new Yemeni counterterrorism unit in the desert, and the Americans were effectively leading the hunt inside the country for Al-Qaeda suspects.[32] However, anti-American sentiment remained as deep as it was widespread in Yemen, as I witnessed in Sanaa when Saddam was arrested by American forces in December 2003. An outraged local in the capital immediately made his way to the historic old town and stabbed the first three Westerners he happened upon. Traffic accidents increased tenfold as frustrated motorists took out their sense of humiliation on one another. My Yemeni Arabic teacher, who often railed against America's role in the region and in particular its invasion of Iraq, had to cancel our class because she was weeping uncontrollably. The local newspapers were full of calls for jihadists to make their way to Iraq.

As though deepening tribal rifts and the consolidation of Al-Qaeda were not bad enough, regional and sectarian divisions in Yemen abound, too. In the years leading up to the Arab Spring, a rebellion led by Hussein Badreddine Al-Huthi, a radical Shiite cleric holed up with as many as 3,000 armed followers in the rugged north near the Saudi border, had left thousands dead and tens of thousands displaced. That is a shockingly high figure even in a region where all males past puberty openly bear arms and violent tribal conflicts are par for the course. A new opposition group was also seeking secession for the south, many of whose people are still deeply resentful at how unification in 1990 had mostly benefited the northern tribal sheikhs who were Saleh's traditional allies. Calling itself the Southern Democratic Assembly, the group's manifesto said it rejected the politics of forced unity and the systematic eradication of the southern identity.[33] In Sanaa, when the high-profile trial of six Al-Qaeda suspects in the October 2000 bombing of the USS *Cole* got under way in 2004, it widened the gap between the pro-American regime and a divided local population seething with anti-American anger following the invasions of Afghanistan and Iraq. A statement on a website that carried extremist Islamic comment threatened to turn Yemen into a "third swamp" for American forces then battling in

Iraq and Afghanistan. The ten-page statement was issued by the Abu Hafs Al-Masri Brigade, another shadowy group that takes its name from a top Al-Qaeda lieutenant who was killed in an American air strike in Afghanistan in 2001, and which had previously claimed responsibility for a number of attacks on Western targets in Yemen.[34] The statement read: "Our goals in the next phase are expanding the circle of conflict by spreading operations all around the world. [We will] drag America into a third swamp—after Iraq and Afghanistan—and let it be Yemen, God willing."[35] In ushering in the Arab Spring, God answered their prayers.

The opening of the USS *Cole* trial coincided with reports of widespread arrests in Sanaa of anti-American preachers and even a senior judge, suspected of backing Huthi's Shiite rebellion in the north. The government accused Huthi, the leader of the Shiite Zaydi sect, of forming an underground armed group and fomenting sectarian strife. Zaydis are a historically moderate Shiite group, living mainly in northwestern Yemen. But Huthi—like his counterpart Moqtada Al-Sadr in Iraq—seemed to have been able to amass in a relatively short time a small army right under the noses of the authorities. Saleh had called on Huthi to turn himself in, promising a fair trial, while damning his followers—known as the "Believing Youth"—for allegedly attacking mosques, urging Yemenis to arm themselves against possible attacks by America, and claiming that democracy in Yemen would bring a Jewish leader to power.[36] When Saleh visited the north, Huthi's followers screamed insults at him, and he had to beat a hasty retreat. As a Shia cleric, Huthi, who was subsequently killed in a battle with Yemeni soldiers, could never have enjoyed widespread support throughout the rest of Yemen, where most of the 60 percent or so of the Sunni population live. However, his anti-Israeli and anti-American rhetoric resonated with almost everyone. The only thing ordinary Yemenis saw as a consequence of its government's alliance with Washington was a worsening economic crisis, the gap between the haves and have-nots increasing, and further social instability—with labor strikes and street riots on the back of price hikes on basic commodities and cuts in fuel subsidies. What was happening in Yemen was a warning from the cradle of the Arab world. Its steadfastly pro-American leader was increasingly losing touch with his youthful, disenfranchised, anti-American population. Radical Islamists of various stripes were filling the vacuum. That was how things stood when the Arab Spring came.

Religious vigilantes emerged. They publicly formed a committee in 2008 to alert police about violations of Islamic law and to help locate places and hunt down people who spread vice. This new group called itself the Committee for the Promotion of Virtue and Prevention of Vice, the exact same name of the official Saudi religious police who, for eight decades, have beaten Saudi citizens into observing prayer times and avoiding the female gaze. The self-appointed head in Yemen was Sheikh Abdul-Majeed Al-Zindani. A Wahhabi cleric, he is the head of Imam University in Sanaa, which is reported as being an infamous breeding ground for extremist students, including the "American Taliban" John Walker Lindh.[37] Al-Zindani is also the sometime spokesman for the Yemeni branch of the Muslim Brotherhood. And he is a vocal supporter of Yemen's main Islamist political party, Islah (Reform), a powerful bloc in the national parliament. The meeting called to found the Committee for the Promotion of Virtue and Prevention of Vice in Yemen drew around 6,000 attendees, mainly tribal and religious leaders but also elected members of parliament. The latter consisted of about 60 Islamists from the Al-Zindani-backed mainstream political group Islah. It simultaneously launched an attack on "spreading moral corruption" in Yemen. The vigilante group insisted that the government take action on mixed dancing, the consumption or sale of alcohol, racy television soap operas, fashion shows, coeducation, pop concerts, women politicians, mannequins displayed in shop windows, and nightclubs of any and all description. Rahma Hugaira, chair of Yemen's Media Women's Forum, summarized the threat these Islamists already posed just before the 2011 uprisings:

> This new vice and virtue movement has the potential to undermine the government. Civil society groups are working hard to modernize society, to establish a social contract grounded in our constitution and reflected in our laws. A group using religion as a weapon threatens all the progress we have achieved.[38]

It threatened, in other words, to turn Yemen into Saudi Arabia, a country that was in an even stronger position to undermine the government when it had effectively ceased functioning. That this new, apparently spontaneous movement against "moral corruption" was named in homage to the Saudi religious police, and headed by a cleric with close religious and financial ties to the Saudi regime, is the heart of the matter. A barely functioning Yemeni state, but with a relatively strong central government, is the

Saudi royal family's preference. That way it poses no threat, has a Washington-aligned (and pro–war on terror) regime, but is easily manipulated. However, for Riyadh a failed state is a nightmare scenario. Nothing if not politically astute, the Saudis appear to have made a move on the vice front in the years leading up to the Arab Spring, not in anticipation of it but with the knowledge that the country was on the verge of collapse anyway. Their hope was that a friendly, reactionary Islamist regime might seize power, and thus facilitate a unifying (and for the Saudis wholly welcome) call for a return to fundamentalist Islam.

Riyadh therefore was perfectly positioned to move when the Yemeni uprising began in 2011. Sheikh Sadeq Al-Ahmar, the overall leader of the Hashid tribal confederation that turned against Saleh, is the son of the late Abdullah bin Hussein Al-Ahmar, who founded the Islamist Islah opposition party. Sadeq's brother, Hamid Al-Ahmar, is a prominent businessman and also a leading member of Islah. Both brothers are known to have links to senior Saudis, as has the powerful General Ali Mohsen Al-Ahmar, who defected to the opposition early on; while Islah itself also reportedly enjoys Saudi patronage.[39] With Saleh in exile in Saudi Arabia, this Riyadh-funded tribal/Islamist alliance hijacked the mass demonstrations in the Yemeni capital. The opposition coalition's most powerful political party, Islah, took day-to-day control of Change Square, the center of the protest movement. Islah was being bankrolled by Hamid Al-Ahmar, the billionaire Hashid tribal confederation leader and leading Islah party figure. The Islah party was "paying to feed the thousands of protesters still living in Change Square. Restaurants surrounding the square have been converted into industrial-sized kitchens with enormous vats of beans, rice and vegetable stew distributed to protesters on a daily basis, all of it funded by Islah."[40] The exhausted liberals, after months of demonstrations and a ruthless crackdown, had all but disappeared. As elsewhere in the Middle East, the Islamists appear to have boundless energy and enthusiasm for their cause, and they are the only ones willing to sacrifice everything in their fight to the bitter end.

All this is good news for Saudi Arabia, and from a war-on-terror perspective for the West, too—at least in the short term. Neither the Hashid tribal confederation nor Islah have any time for Al-Qaeda. But neither do they have any time for democracy, and they have still less for freedom of speech and cultural expression. Yemeni national unity remains an even more distant dream. In August 2011, the Yemeni opposition finally established a National Council as an alternative to the Saleh regime. Just one day later, at least 23 of its 143 members had resigned, including most of the Islah members. Their gripe? The council lacked balance between members from southern and northern provinces.[41] Saleh had meanwhile returned to Yemen, but having been given refuge by the Saudis, he too was more indebted to them than ever. As Yemen teetered on civil war, the Saudis had all eventualities covered.

YEMEN'S USEFULNESS AND IMPORTANCE, like Bahrain's, is its strategically crucial location. But neither country has a significant oil reserve, while Libya does. This allowed the Saudis to make a deal with Washington: Let us invade Bahrain and we will vote for U.N. Resolution 1973, which kick-started the NATO intervention in Libya by authorizing "all necessary force" to protect civilians.[42] America needed Saudi support for the resolution. This way, Obama could present his Libya war as a humanitarian mission, rather than yet another oil grab, into which he had been half-dragged by his insistent European allies. With Saudi help, it had the cover of all freedom-loving Arabs in the form of support from the dinosaur institution called the Arab League. What really mattered to Washington was the security of its naval base in Bahrain. Under no circumstances could it risk letting the tiny island fall under Iranian influence, as would have been inevitable had the Shia-led rising succeeded there. The Americans and Saudis were greatly helped in their ruse by the fact that only half of the twenty-two Arab League members were present at the vote supporting NATO action, and six of the eleven that voted were members of the same Gulf Cooperation Council that had been itching to invade Bahrain.[43] For the Saudis, it was an easy decision to sell out Colonel Gaddafi in return for containing Shia-dominated Iran, protecting America's naval base in Bahrain, and ensuring Washington would turn a blind eye to its suppression of Shia protests in its own Eastern Province. There had been numerous reports over the years that Gaddafi had tried to assassinate King Abdullah, and the two leaders had famously engaged in a slanging match at an Arab League summit in 2002 (resulting in the live feed being cut). Moreover, having been at the helm of a tribal country themselves for eight decades, the Al-Saud knew that an uprising in Libya would descend into civil war and perpetual intertribal clashes. What better way of demonstrating that a far more preferable course than revolt and mayhem was the status quo?

When civil war subsequently broke out in Libya, that country also split along tribal lines. Even some major oilfields quickly fell into the hands of armed local tribesmen. If Libya is again to be unified—and that, as in Yemen, remains a huge if—it will only be possible under the leadership of a tribal council posing as a national government, which will have to appease demands for an Islamist state by the jihadists they fought alongside to oust Colonel Gaddafi. As the West became ever more deeply embroiled in its Libyan misadventure, it became clear that it, and its latest Coalition of the Willing, was deliberately defending and arming a rabble called the "eastern rebels" that included not only unruly tribal gangs but also countless Islamist extremists. Gaddafi's son, Saif Al-Islam, said in the middle of the civil war that he had made contact with Islamists among the rebels and that the government would announce an alliance with them. "The liberals will escape or be killed," he declared. "We will do it together. . . . Libya will look like Saudi Arabia, Iran. So what?" he added. "I know they are terrorists. They are bloody. They are not nice. But you have to accept them."[44] It came to nothing. But in a nutshell, that from the outset was also NATO's attitude. In Libya, the West has repeated the deadly mistake it made in Afghanistan and Iraq: arming fanatical jihadists and tribesmen. Sooner or later, they will turn against their paymaster.

Nobody had thought there was any organized opposition to Colonel Gaddafi, apart from the radical Islamists he had arrested and imprisoned. Even when the rebellion began in the eastern city of Benghazi, little ground was directly seized by them. Much of its gains was due to the defection of Gaddafi's forces in the area, who yielded to persuasive arguments of family and tribal affiliation. As time passed, less appeared to be certain about the rebels, to judge from the flood of newspaper reports, except that they were disorganized, shot in the air, and did a great deal of running away[45]—all useful tactics, we are told, in guerrilla warfare, but perhaps less so when your NATO-sanctioned guardian angel expects you to roll up the country from east to west like a carpet. "It could be a very big surprise when Gaddafi leaves and we find out who we are really dealing with," was how one American academic summed up the situation.[46]

A big surprise when Gaddafi leaves? As anyone who read *The Wall Street Journal* on April 2, 2011, would have discovered, one of the rebels' commanders, Abdel Hakim Al-Hasidi (also known as Abdel Hakim Belhaj), had been a member of the Libyan Islamic Fighting Group (LIFG) since the 1990s.[47] The LIFG is a violent jihadist outfit that, for decades, waged a holy war against the Gaddafi regime with an aim of creating an Islamic state. It was banned worldwide after the September 11 attacks,[48] when Al-Hasidi, its leader, went to Afghanistan. He frankly admits that he recruited dozens of Al-Qaeda members to the insurgent cause in Iraq, too, where the LIFG made up the second largest group of foreign fighters (after those from the terrorist heartland of Saudi Arabia). Many of them, he adds, joined the rebellion in Libya.[49] For Al-Hasidi, his fighters in Libya "are patriots and good Muslims," but Al-Qaeda men "are also good Muslims and are fighting against the invader" in Iraq.[50]

During the uprising, the LIFG morphed into the Derna Brigade, one of many Islamist militias that goes by the official name of the Martyrs of Abu Salim Brigade. Abu Salim is a prison in Tripoli and was the site of a 1996 prison massacre of as many as 1,200 Islamist political prisoners. Derna is a town near Benghazi, and like the latter city is a center of Islamic resistance dating back to the anticolonial struggle against the Italians. It was the main recruiting ground for jihadists who made their way to Afghan to fight the Soviets in the 1980s, and when they returned home, they staged an uprising against the Gaddafi regime in the 1990s. A massive clampdown followed, which culminated in the massacre in Abu Salim prison, which in turn led to the NATO-backed rebel uprising that finally ousted Gaddafi.

The Libyan revolution started when families of the victims of that massacre demonstrated against the repeated arrest of a lawyer in early 2011 who had been representing them.[51] The locals of Benghazi joined the rebellion out of tribal hatred for Gaddafi, who in turn hated the rebellious city to the extent that he referred to it as the Old Hag.[52] NATO's toppling of the Gaddafi regime was achieved with the help of rebel fighters on the ground motivated by religious and tribal animosity, not a longing for a British parliamentary system. When Gaddafi gave an interview to three Western reporters shortly after the uprising against him began, he repeatedly referred to it, to the endless mockery of Western commentators, as an Al-Qaeda-led rebellion.[53] For all of his craziness, he was in this instance spot on. The "rebels" were religious extremists fighting to impose Islamic law in Libya once secular Gaddafi was ousted. "An Al-Qaeda leader of Libyan origin, Abu

Yahya Al-Libi, released a statement backing the insurrection a week ago," *The London Telegraph* reported at the time, "while Yusuf Qaradawi, the Qatar-based, Muslim Brotherhood-linked theologian issued a fatwa authorizing Col Gaddafi's military entourage to assassinate him."[54]

When NATO launched its campaign in March 2011, opinion was divided as to how effective they would be in forcing Gaddafi from power. But there was one aspect of the campaign on which all observers agreed: the loyalty pledged to one side or the other by the country's more than 2,000 notoriously fickle, ancient tribes would ultimately determine the war's duration and outcome. Just as important, it would also determine what would happen after one side had at least nominally defeated the other. Not that the question of who was fighting on whose side was ever easy to answer when it comes to Libya's civil war. The Islamist militias had fought alongside the tribes, but independently, in the sense that they refuse to accept anyone else's ultimate authority. And like paid mercenaries in wartime, Arab tribes are in the habit of switching allegiances on a whim. Ultimately, they have no loyalty to anyone either, other than to their fellow clansmen. And they pour scorn on the concept of a nation-state. Only a fool would bet on their long-term allegiances or consider them a unifying national force. And only a buffoon would expect them to embrace Western democratic principles. Not the least of their problems is that they quickly get sidetracked by revenge attacks on each other to settle ancient feuds or to respond to a new (real or perceived) slight on their honor.

For Libya's powerful Obeidi tribe, which was among the first to join the anti-Gaddafi alliance, maintaining honor was always paramount. For them there could have been no greater provocation than the assassination of their leader, Abdel Fatah Younis, in July 2011. His death signaled the beginning of intertribal civil war in the country. Once a powerful interior minister under Gaddafi, in February 2011 Younis defected to the rebels and became their star army commander. Initially there was euphoria in the Western media—it really did not take much to cause that—when his tribe, and other key tribes, defected. It was at best premature and at worst naïve. NATO's military campaign slogan from the outset might have been: My Enemy's Enemy Is My Friend. It tried to woo key rebel tribes like the Obeidi into an unlikely alliance with radical jihadists and pro-democracy liberals, the two other groups NATO was also arming to the teeth. The tribes' incentive was a share in the country's vast oil wealth, once a new Western-backed regime was installed. The jihadists wanted revenge against Gaddafi for his decades of persecution and the imposition of Islamic law. The liberals—always the most vulnerable group in these circumstances—hoped that, out of the chaos, a democracy would somehow emerge, which would lead to the establishment of a secular civil state—and in the initial enthusiasm about the rebels' seizure of Tripoli, the capital, that is what they confidently declared would happen.

Militarily, the strategy of recruiting the tribes seemed strikingly successful. The million-strong Warfala, Libya's biggest tribe (accounting for one-sixth of the nation's total population), soon joined the anti-Gaddafi alliance. That gave the revolutionary opposition crucial support in its strongholds of Tripoli and Benghazi, the country's two biggest cities (the latter having become the rebels' de facto capital). The Warfala tribe's defection was followed by the Tarhuna tribe, which also has about a million members. But Younis's death saw NATO's political strategy begin to unravel even as massive military gains continued to go to the rebels. He was shot dead with two aides, also from the Obeidi tribe, after being summoned to Benghazi by the Western-backed National Transitional Council (NTC). Nobody knew who was responsible. But the fact that their bodies were mutilated led some to suggest it had all the hallmarks of a classic tribal revenge killing. Others pointed the finger at the Islamists ostensibly fighting alongside the rebels. It is true that the Islamists are hardly averse to mutilating corpses. And they had the clear incentive of murdering a former interior minister who had been responsible for arresting and torturing their rank-and-file members for decades. The Obeidi quickly rejected an offer of an investigation into Younis's death by the NTC, instead predictably deciding to take the law into their own hands. "We will leave it to the tribe to bring us justice," Younis's son threatened, hours after his tribal followers went on a gun-firing rampage.[55] The entire NTC cabinet was then sacked, meaning that the only way for the rebels to maintain a semblance of unity was to have no civil leadership at all. Other opposition groups and tribes soon began to seek to foment discord among the rebels' ranks to further their own competing agendas. Not that NATO strategy had until that point managed to achieve anything other than encouraging superficial unity among the ramshackle rebels. Even before Younis's assassination, rebels from the besieged city of Misrata were refusing to join ranks with revolutionaries from Benghazi, because of different tribal affiliations. Different tribal factions *within* Misrata were also at each other's throats, because of a historic feud between the local Misratans and other locals known as Tawerghans. Fighters from the rebel-aligned Zintan tribe, instead of fighting Gaddafi's forces head-on, took up arms specifically against the pro-government Mashashya tribe, again taking advantage of the chaos to settle old scores.

This is a taste of the way Libya will be ruled in the future, when these rebel groups attain national power. And from all of this it will be clear why the only way Gaddafi was able to rule Libya for decades was by playing a skillful game of tribal repression and coercion. He tried to undermine tribal alliances through intermarriage, modernization, urbanization, and a sense of national pride deriving from the anticolonial war that brought independence and him to power. The tragic irony of the Libyan civil war is that the tribes, and their byzantine web of links and rivalries, once again became central to the fate of the country. As did the once-repressed radical jihadists, who were either released by Gaddafi in the initial stages of the war (as an attempt to appease the opposition) or broke out of jail. The tribes' lack of unity, along with inevitable splits between the liberals and Islamists and within the various Islamist ranks, is what for months gave Gaddafi the motivation to refuse to enter into a negotiated settlement.

NATO's bungling campaign, including the killing of large numbers of civilians and the inevitable destruction of civilian infrastructure, could only ever hope to achieve, at best, replacing the Gaddafi regime with an Islamist-infiltrated tribal council, with the liberals marginalized if not slaughtered. Or, alternatively, to throw the Gaddafi regime (or what was left of it) into the arms of the Islamists.

In August 2011, in a sober essay questioning the still dominant Arab Spring narrative, George Friedman, founder of the intelligence think tank Stratfor, offered a more realistic assessment of the Libyan quagmire than was generally available at the time. Regime change there is "not going to be clearly victorious," he explained. But even if it is, it is "not going to be clearly democratic." And if democratic, it "is obviously not going to be liberal." The myth, he concluded, "that beneath every Libyan is a French republican yearning to breathe free is dubious in the extreme."[56] Abdel-Jalil, the Libyan rebel leader, said a week after Friedman's essay appeared that his opposition forces had chosen to start their first attack on Tripoli on the twentieth day of Ramadan, which marks the ancient Islamic Battle of Badr (when Muslims first fought for the holy city of Mecca in 624).[57] That fact hardly inspires confidence in a secular, liberal future for Libya. The one certainty is that the tribes' loyalty is there to be bought by the highest bidder and always will be. This is why, as the political alliance was falling apart along tribal lines and Gaddafi's son was wooing the jihadists, Gaddafi repeatedly called for his loyal tribes to return to the fold in the face of foreign "aggression" and "imperialism." He was evoking the colonial days, when the tribes, along with the Islamists, were key to achieving victory in the war of independence against Italy. Little noticed in the West, but presumably avidly read by Gaddafi himself at the time, was the manifesto issued in July 2011, just before the rebels took Tripoli, by the Libyan Tribal Council, which represents all the tribes who in post-Gaddafi Libya will have to be pacified. It read in part:

> The Tribal Council condemns the crusader aggression on the Great Republic executed by the NATO and the Arab regressive forces, which is a grave threat to Libyan civilians as it continues to kill them as NATO bombs civilian targets. We do not and will not accept any authority other than the authority that we chose with our free will which is the People's Congress and Peoples Committees, and the popular social leadership. . . . We intend to oppose with all the means available to us the NATO crusader aggressors and their appointed lackeys.[58]

They were not much covered in the West, either, but during the NATO bombing campaign, there were regular huge rallies in Tripoli against the Western aggression and in support of Gaddafi.[59] Despite not having been given any legal authorization to do so by any international body, the final rebel assault on Tripoli was carried out with the crucial help of Western special forces, both in terms of the fighting on the ground and in the military training the rebels received beforehand.[60] This was needed because Western leaders, including Obama, were given to saying at the outset that Gaddafi would be gone within weeks if not days; they misjudged the effectiveness of military intervention. They also misjudged the huge levels of support Gaddafi enjoyed in the capital. He had poured huge funds from his oil wealth into his main center of power. The people of Tripoli did not rise up against him. A few thousand of the city's 2 million inhabitants welcomed the rebels. In the future, large numbers of those who did not are unlikely to embrace unquestioningly a transparently foreign-backed transitional council, whose main job is to sell off the country's resources to the highest bidders from France, Britain, Italy, and the United States.

Within a week of the fall of Tripoli, Western companies were already scrambling for domination of the country's oil industries. China and Russia—who refused to back the NATO campaign—were shut out from the start.[61] The campaign therefore achieved what it set out to: steal the country's oil. Strictly in those terms, Libya might just be a success story, following the Iraq model. A governing body will be made up of pro-West former Gaddafi henchmen protected by Western powers and suddenly richer and more powerful than they could ever have dreamed. As in Iraq, the price will be the sacrifice of Libya's once-secular political system. Libya will become far more conservative, and the Muslim Brotherhood—along with more extremist Salafis—will dominate the political scene, with endless funding from the Wahhabi Persian Gulf state of Qatar that backed the rebels from the start.[62] This will not bother the West, which has been cozying up to the fanatical Wahhabis of Saudi Arabia for eight decades and is negotiating once again with the Taliban in Afghanistan. That strongly suggests that Libya is not on the road to a Western democracy, any more than are Saudi Arabia or Afghanistan. As in post-Saddam Iraq, Libya will, to be sure, have the superficial trappings of democracy. Elections will be celebrated by the Western media as though they marked the Second Coming, as the Western-backed candidates will be ensured victory through massive funding and sleek advertising campaigns orchestrated by an army of Western advisers swarming the city like flies. It is worth remembering what the U.S. general Anthony Zinni said by way of summarizing the attitude of the Iraq war's orchestrators amid the chaos that engulfed that country after the war officially ended: "Maybe some strong man emerges, it fractures, and there really is a Kurdish state. Who cares? There's some bloodshed and it's messy. Who cares? I mean, we've taken out Saddam. We've asserted our strength in the Middle East."[63]

Again, as in Iraq, the real war began in Libya after the West declared its mission accomplished. Libya's elaborate system of tribal patronage and rivalries and its Islamist militias mean a national unity government will find it difficult, if not impossible, to remain credible in the eyes of ordinary Libyans. The bigger tribes will continue to battle each other for greater influence. The defeated tribes, with nothing to lose, will launch an eternal war of revenge. The liberals will realize that they have no constituency to speak of inside this deeply reactionary Bedouin country and will be tarnished by their association with the Western powers who bombed their country to smithereens under the pretext of liberating it. Once the euphoria dies down, the slow, painful process of rebuilding the country will also be hindered by endemic corruption and nepotism. Sooner or later, the Islamists will fill the vacuum, and not for a millisecond will they relent in their demand for an Islamist state. The national government will have to cede to that demand, and will in fact enthusiastically embrace it as a way of publicly distancing themselves from the Western thugs who installed them and continue to prop them up. Even before Tripoli fell, the rebel-led transitional council had issued a draft constitution that clearly stated that Islamic law would be "the principal source of legislation" in their new Arab haven for freedom and liberty.[64] By October 2011, Salafis had destroyed dozens of gravestones around Tripoli, saying they are a form of idolatry that violates Islamic law.

And when Gaddafi was caught, his treatment at the hands of the rabble who found him hardly suggested that Libya had turned a page for the better. After being tortured and sodomized with a stick, he was executed in cold blood. A few days later, Libya's interim leader declared annulment of all laws that contravened sharia.

FOUR

THE SHIA AXIS

IRAN AND SAUDI ARABIA ARE BRUTAL MILITARY STATES OVERRUN BY secret police and ruled by a small clique of vicious old men who wrap themselves in the cloak of religion. The most politically influential and militarily powerful countries in the Middle East, they are also the most culturally restrictive, socially oppressive, and institutionally theocratic; and they are also equally hell-bent on stamping out moderation and common sense, not just at home but also abroad. The region's stubborn refusal to embrace democracy and pluralism can be understood in geopolitical terms partly as a result of the perpetual, if low-key, conflict between these two Islamist regimes. If the Arab Spring had even a remote chance of ushering in a wave of progressive change, it would have had to challenge, in concrete and progressive ways, the internal power structures and regionwide influence of both countries. A tall order indeed.

Instead, the opposite occurred. The Iranian and Saudi regimes nipped in the bud their own brief and very limited unrest, then exploited the turmoil to further their geopolitical reach. The last thing either country wants is to face off directly against the other in a war, so for decades Lebanon has provided a faraway playground for them to test each other's strength through their Sunni and Shia proxies there. When the Shia rebellion in northern Yemen broke out, Saudi Arabia bombed them with the Yemeni government's blessing while Iran was arming them on the ground.[1] The Arab Spring allowed for the extension of this great game to Bahrain and then to Syria. Even if regime change comes to either of those two countries, the vacuum will not be filled by the highly disorganized pro-democracy campaigners. Instead, as in Tunisia and Egypt, an odd partnership of firebrand Islamists and old-style authoritarians will emerge; and to further their markedly different, but ultimately compatible, agendas, they will eagerly bend over backward to do the bidding of their new antidemocratic paymasters in the Persian Gulf.

Much as in Saudi Arabia, the power of Iran's regime comes from oil money, an extensive repressive security apparatus and, for the most part, a deeply reactionary and compliant population. This last point is especially important. Most Westerners understand these countries through their own journalists and pro-democracy activists, who obsessively home in on an English-speaking, liberal elite. There is no great conspiracy at play. It is just that most of them do not speak the local languages and, whenever possible, understandably prefer to avoid government-appointed minders and translators. Even if they do know better, they have little choice but to provide the "they want to be free like us" copy their editors back home demand. The overwhelming impression is that the Iranian and Saudi masses have a deep thirst for Western freedoms. I have lived in Saudi Arabia and traveled extensively through Iran, and the reality in both countries struck me as markedly different from the accepted view. Most of the people are silent for a reason. They have no time for the handful of liberals who live in their midst more or less unseen. The liberals in turn resent them. The education that makes a liberal—a liberal education—must be sought abroad and is therefore rarely available to the masses in these countries. Even those in Saudi Arabia who can afford to send their children overseas often have no idea how to choose a school in, say, Hoboken, New Jersey, wisely, and often their children return with a rudimentary command of MTV or ghetto speak but are barely able to spell their own name in either their own language or English. If anything, they have even fewer ideas in their heads than when they set out.

Unfortunately, the masses get exercised over trivia: caricatures of the Prophet, an allegedly blasphemous passage in an otherwise unread book, or some perceived slight or other to the Quran. As a result, they do not rise up to demand democracy or a fair trial in a court of law for the offenders behind these supposed crimes, but bay for the blood of the accursed infidels, not least because it offers them a rare opportunity to work off their frustrations in the only kind of demonstration their governments smile on indulgently.

Iran and Saudi Arabia have high levels of unemployment and poverty, and are profoundly corrupt, but they remain able to throw a great deal of financial heft behind exporting their uniquely skewered brands of radical Islamism. Again, that is because they maintain some kind of legitimacy at home as defenders of the faith. Hardline scholars have indoctrinated their populations with the idea that Islam forbids rebellion unless the country's leader can be proved an infidel. And the opposition in both countries is invariably even more hardline than the regimes.

In the case of Saudi Arabia, the opposition is made up of clerics who want an even more fundamentalist state and accuse the regime of having corrupted the kingdom with Western decadent norms.[2] In Iran there is the more vibrant Green Movement, an opposition that in 2009 briefly claimed the streets. But it is no less Islamist than the Saudi opposition. The obsession of the Western press with Twitterbabble in English made it look as though the Green Movement was a youthful block party trying to turn Tehran into the Middle East's version of Barcelona. But Mir Hosein Mousavi, the opposition leader whose failed presidential bid sparked the protests, is actually, as I understand it, as hardline as the hardliners. He believes that the Iranian clerical elite betrayed the revolutionary ideals of Ayatollah Khomeini, the apple of whose eye and designated successor he had once been.[3] A liberal, of course, would argue the exact opposite: that Khomeini had betrayed the revolutionaries' ideals by killing them and then establishing a medieval theocracy. Like Rachid Ghannouchi, the leader of Tunisia's Ennahda party, Mousavi favors dark suits and a trimmed beard and likes to talk in rousing terms about democracy. In my opinion his preferred version of democracy, too, would be no less extreme than the kind Ghannouchi wants to impose in Tunisia. In fact, it would be an austere Islamic state. Mousavi, then, did not choose green as the color of the movement because he hoped to preside over a merry band of progressive ecowarriors. In the Middle East, the color green has quite another connotation. Those who still cannot work out what it is should perhaps Google "Saudi Arabian flag."

Both the Iranian and Saudi regimes tirelessly interfere in other countries' internal affairs, and they openly or clandestinely support murderous jihadists outside their borders. The irony is that although Tehran and Riyadh are so similar, they loathe one another. And they have diametrically opposite relations with the West. In no small part, this is because of the historic Sunni-Shia animosity outlined in the previous chapter. But nowhere is their eternal sectarian conflict more bizarrely complicated than in their different attitudes toward Israel and its ally America. The Saudi royal family's education system spews out a kind of anti-Semitic hatred not known since the Nazis.[4] But Riyadh works hard to maintain the status quo vis-à-vis Israel, which would therefore be happy for the Saudi ruling family to rule forever. Washington indulges the Saudis as well because, for all their sponsorship of anti-Semitic bile, they pose no threat to the Jewish state so long as they keep their military leaders and citizens in line. Thus, neither Washington nor Tel Aviv has any interest in pushing Riyadh to implement democratic change. Iran, despite having a protected Jewish minority (do not believe the propaganda that the Jews are oppressed), and for the most part since the 1979 revolution eschewing the kind of crude anti-Semitism of the Wahhabis, is under its current president Mahmood Ahmadinejad openly committed to Israel's destruction and given to holding conferences on how the Holocaust did not take place. The Iranian population, too, would cheer such an event all the way. Many of Iran's fanatical Revolutionary Guards and clerics would probably die for the privilege of making it happen. Washington and Tel Aviv therefore endlessly criticize the Iranian regime's record on human rights and restrictions on democracy and free expression, even as they remain silent about Saudi Arabia's arguably much worse record.

As a result, Saudi Arabia is securely locked into a symbiotic relationship with the United States, which offers Riyadh military and political support in return for a secure supply of oil, support for its wars and billions of dollars in arms purchases, and the understanding that only token gestures of support will be forthcoming for the Palestinians' right to statehood. Iran is more vulnerable to America, although the invasion of Iraq complicated matters. Iraq is an American puppet *and* an Iranian client state. Its democratically elected prime minister and Washington favorite, Nouri Al-Maliki, considers himself a deputy of the Iranian regime.[5] If push came to shove, it would be very difficult to predict which way the country would turn in this tug-of-war. In case the West and Iran seriously come to blows, graduating from their perpetual low-level bickering and mutual denunciations to some kind of warfare, the Iranians could cause huge damage to American interests in Iraq, whose Shia-majority population comprises mostly followers of Moqtada Al-Sadr, among the most anti-Western cleric in the country. As a foreign-policy operation, then, Iraq was an even greater disaster for America than many already believe, as it is now Iran's only trump card apart from its proxy Hizbollah in Lebanon. Like Libya's Colonel Gaddafi, Saddam Hussein was, for all of his clearly demonstrated madness, contained, and so presented no threat to anyone outside his own country. A decade on, the overthrow of Saddam has led to a much clearer and ever present danger to America's strategic position. Iraq, though, was still so mired in its own postinvasion quagmire early in 2011 that no more than a few thousand protestors took to the country's streets during the Arab Spring. However, with the ascendancy of Islamism in Turkey, Tehran finds itself subject to a kind of pincer movement of Sunni extremism. This is forcing the Iranian regime to redouble efforts in support of its proxies abroad: Hezbollah in Lebanon and, more pressingly, the Assad regime in Syria.

THE IRAN-HEZBOLLAH-SYRIA AXIS became evident when swift and decisive help came to Syrian dictator Bashir Al-Assad after an uprising erupted against him. The first reports of Iranian and Hezbollah intervention were from Daraa, a city of some 75,000 in southwestern Syria—a region suffering from a prolonged drought.[6] Together with the provincial cities of Hama and Homs, it soon became a center of the antiregime protests. Protestors said they heard southern Lebanese accents and Farsi, the language of Iran, spoken among many pro-regime forces who attacked them, indicating they may have been from Hezbollah and Iran.[7] The opposition Reform Party of Syria similarly claimed that Iran's notorious Revolutionary Guard had taken over a military base in Homs. One of the party's leaders claimed Syrian forces were even being commanded by the Revolutionary Guard. "Syria has become the thirty-second province of Iran," he declared.[8] The media-savvy, Western-based Syrian opposition parties have their own agendas. They know that linking Iran to the violence of the Syrian regime can do no harm in the propaganda wars if the listeners are Americans. At the same time, it is true that Iran offered Syria a $5.8 billion aid package to bail out the regime in the wake of the economic fallout from the uprising, a gesture that reportedly had the backing of the country's spiritual leader, Ayatollah Khamenei; and Tehran also provided Syria with 290,000 barrels of oil a day free of charge.[9] In March 2011, Turkey revealed concrete evidence of Iranian intervention in Syria. It told the U.N. Security Council that it had intercepted a massive arms cache on an Iranian cargo plane destined for Syria that included Kalashnikovs, machine guns, huge amounts of ammunition, and mortar shells.[10]

Hassan Nasrallah, the popular the leader of the Lebanese Shia resistance group Hezbollah and a close ally of both Syria and Iran, meanwhile made a televised speech calling on Syrians to back Assad and demanding that Arab nations reject sanctions imposed by the West on the Syrian regime over the killing of protestors. "We call on all Syrians to preserve their country as well as the ruling regime, a regime of resistance, and to give their leaders a chance to cooperate with all Syria's communities in order to implement the necessary reforms," he said. "The difference between the Arab uprisings and Syria . . . is that President Assad is convinced that reforms are necessary, unlike Bahrain and other Arab countries."[11] Nasrallah was capitalizing on his massive popularity among the grassroots in the Arab world; they see him as a beacon of this "resistance" he speaks of to the Washington-Tel Aviv nexus, a nexus that the Arab street has long been accustomed to blaming for all its troubles. But instead, Nasrallah ended up showing his true colors as a faithful Tehran lackey.

Bashir Al-Assad comes from the Baath party. Its philosophy is a mix of Arab nationalism and crude socialism, and it rules Syria with an iron fist. It is the most intrusive police state of the Arab world, and there has been a state of emergency in place since 1963. Just like the imagery of Big Brother, posters with the face of the president—a dictator so utterly lacking in charisma that he almost makes one long for the days of Idi Amin—can be found on every street corner. Anyone using an internet café has to provide full personal details, and all his online activity is monitored. Television and the press are strictly controlled by the state. All newspapers are government-approved. Yet like Tunisia, Syria embraces an odd paradox. The secularist Baathist regime tolerates personal liberties including alcohol, gambling, and prostitution. Men and boys openly cruise one another in the cafés and parks of Damascus, one of the most socially liberal cities in the Middle East.[12] The Islamists are given no role in the political affairs of the state. All of which begs the question: What makes this secular regime so dear to the mullahs of Tehran?

The main reason, of course, is political expediency: Syria is a conduit for arms supplies from Iran to Hezbollah in Lebanon and Hamas in the Gaza Strip. But another is that Syria is dominated by an obscure sect called the Alawites. They are named after Ali, the fourth and last of the so-called rightly guided caliphs who ruled after the Prophet Mohammed, and he is revered by the Shia. That is why the Alawites are often described as an "offshoot" of Shia Islam, although even other Shia can regard them as heretics and infidels. Their faith is secretive, passed on in whispers from generation to generation, but is thought to include elements of Christianity, such as worship of the Trinity and celebration of Christmas. The Alawites, who endured centuries of persecution under the Ottomans, historically have been concentrated in the coastal Mediterranean areas of Syria. These days, they make up a minority of at most 15 percent of Syria's total population, while 70 percent are Sunni and the rest are mainly Christians. But the Assads are Alawites, as are most of their leading strongmen in the army and security forces. For decades the Alawites have presented their secular rule—not inaccurately—as a bulwark against the sectarian disintegration of the country and as a means of pacifying those who fear that they want to impose their religion on the majority. Only by propping up the insular, secular Alawites—so the regime's massive security apparatus is trained to believe—can Syria be prevented from splitting along tribal and sectarian lines, and consequently descending into bloody civil war. This self-fulfilling prophecy of sectarian strife partly explains why the overwhelmingly Sunni security apparatus remained staunchly behind Assad in the first six months of protests against his regime. The only serious challenge to Assad the Elder's rule had been an uprising in the city of Hama in 1982, which was led by the extremist Muslim Brotherhood. The result was the epic massacre of anywhere between 17,000 and 40,000 insurgents and the razing of the city, perhaps the most barbaric act of repression ever perpetrated by a modern Arab government against its own people. That massacre accounted for much of the anger during the 2011 protests in the same city, just as Gaddafi's massacre of Islamists at Abu Salim prison in Tripoli in 1992 galvanized their relatives to rise up against him.

The Hama massacre was also the most shocking example of how the Syrian regime has used this constant fear of sectarian strife, or of an Islamist takeover, to justify a draconian crackdown on the opposition. As in Egypt and Tunisia, the excesses and abuses of the secular regime only succeeded in giving secularism itself a bad name and, by extension, giving credence to the Islamist argument that godlessness was the cause of all the country's problems. For decades, it failed to nurture the imagination of young people with anything but dim-witted propaganda. The result was that fundamentalist Islam grew from the obsession of a few thousand straggly-bearded crackpots a few decades ago into the sole respectable political alternative many Syrians are now capable of imagining.

In Syria around 30 to 40 percent of urban women are now veiled, while in the countryside almost all women are completely covered in black, Wahhabi style.[13] This was unheard-of a decade ago. Indeed, the full-face-covering *niqab* used to be forbidden in schools, universities, and public places. In July 2011, at the height of the protests, that ban was lifted, and the country's only casino was also shut down.[14] At the beginning of the uprising against him, Assad vacillated between concessions and an ever more brutal crackdown. Islamic political prisoners were released from jails as a gesture of goodwill[15]—but, as in Libya, the move appears to have backfired as the newly freed radicals became active in the antigovernment insurgency. But Assad knows that the Islamists are his most powerful and determined enemies. There was an increasing Islamist and sectarian flavor to the protests, all assurances by the protestors' Facebook spokesmen to the contrary. Some Alawites were chased down and killed by an enraged Sunni mob in Homs; and Christians in the same city said that, although they had initially been in favor of the protests, they were now backing government forces after witnessing examples of sectarian strife that made them afraid for their own lives.[16] One slogan shouted by demonstrators in April 2011 in the city of Qamishli was "Alawis to the grave and Christians to Beirut."[17] Non-Sunnis were driven out of the town of Jisr Al-Shugour. And while arms and personnel support perhaps flowed to the Syrian regime from Iran and Hezbollah, extremist, violent Sunni terrorists, who were increasingly mingling with the protestors, were getting their own arms supplies via Lebanon and Turkey.[18] This is why there were mass rallies in support of the regime in Damascus and Syria's second city of Aleppo, which for the first six months of the uprising did not witness major antiregime protests.[19] The pro-Assad demonstrators may have had no love for the cucumber-faced leader or his henchmen, but they valued the secularism of his rule and feared the consequences of an Islamist takeover if his regime fell.

Assad, though, showed no intention of giving up power. Events at the time of writing suggest he will find other means through which to try to stop dissent—and that will chiefly mean the use of violence against his own people. Seeing that his concessions to the Islamist grassroots failed to produce the desired effect, he seems to have decided to go for broke. Government forces cracked down on protestors with redoubled force. In early

August 2011, they bombed the city of Deir Al-Zour, killing at least 42 people, and cut off electricity to the Islamist stronghold of Hama, which, since it became a focal point for the protests (as in 1982), had existed in a constant state of siege. It was then that the unflinching, principled champions of freedom and democracy, the Saudi royal family, made their move. In a bold gesture, Riyadh recalled its ambassador to Damascus. "What is happening in Syria is not acceptable for Saudi Arabia," King Abdullah thundered in a statement. "Syria should think wisely before it's too late and issue and enact reforms that are not merely promises but actual reforms," he said. "Either it chooses wisdom on its own or it will be pulled down into the depths of turmoil and loss."[20] That statement was the moment when the Arab Spring descended into farce. The House of Saud's call on the Syrian regime to implement serious reforms and respect human rights was the most preposterous smokescreen yet for more geopolitical maneuvering. The Saudis meant to isolate Syria, Iran's only Arab ally, while emboldening the Sunni opposition within Syria itself in anticipation of the eventual ouster of Assad and his minority Alawite-dominated elite. The uprising seems to have had genuinely popular roots, drawing people from all walks of life onto the streets in many of the less developed regions. But by the time Riyadh withdrew its ambassador, it knew that other similarly popular Arab uprisings—from Tunisia and Egypt to Yemen—had paved the way, however inadvertently, for the Islamists to emerge as the dominant force. All it needed to do was co-opt them. A post-Assad Syria would likely follow the same pattern, and Riyadh was poised to align itself with a new Sunni-led, more anti-Iran government in Damascus.

Such an eventuality would not be bad news for Washington. Saudi Arabia has, as we have seen, always gladly done America's bidding in the region. The Saudis would like Syria to be smoothly taken over by the Sunni majority. Even in the unlikely event that it happened smoothly, yet another Saudi-backed takeover by the Muslim Brotherhood and its more extremist Sunni allies would be an impediment to the spread of democracy. The collapse of the Syrian regime would mean the end of a brutal dictatorship—as did the Iraq invasion for the apologists of the Bush "doctrine"—but it would also mean the end of the only remaining secular Arab country, and thus for secularism in the Arab world.

Washington, as ever, lined up with the Saudis against Iran. After his loyal Saudi servant had laid the groundwork by withdrawing his ambassador from Damascus, Obama, in a joint statement with President Nicolas Sarkozy of France and Chancellor Angela Merkel of Germany, declared that Assad "must" resign. The leaders of the free world justified their edict by citing "widespread condemnation" from other Arab rulers—who had followed Riyadh's lead and not-so-subtle pressure in withdrawing their ambassadors from Damascus.[21] The result of this stunning display of international statesmanship, of course, was that Assad was driven even deeper into a corner. The next day, he went on television to warn countries "close and far away"—apparently to include Islamist-ruled Turkey, which played host to the Syrian opposition—against an intervention that he said "will have huge consequences that they will never tolerate."[22] The Syrian president may well cling to office through sheer authoritarianism, his army having regained control through massacre and menace; but it will then have to exist under crippling Western sanctions, becoming ever more dependent on its sole ally in Tehran. Alternatively, the country could descend into drawn-out, blood-soaked civil war—as happened to neighboring Lebanon in the 1970s. As in that terrible war, conflict in Syria would in all likelihood be extraordinarily savage. Given the media blackout, nobody in the West knows, with any level of certainly, what was really going on inside Syria in 2011, except that many innocent civilians were slaughtered. Without reliable information and access, Western reporters as usual relied on English-language Twitter feeds, which could originate from anywhere and are hardly likely to represent the vox populi of an Arabic-speaking country.

The rise of Islamism in Syria would also be a major threat to Israel. Again, there is a paradox here, in that the Baath regime has indulged in anti-Israel rhetoric but in practice has done little: since 1967, it has not fired a single shot in Israel's direction. Technically, Syria has been at war with Israel since then, but its bellicose stance has mainly been used to justify the state of emergency in Syria itself. Anti-Zionist rhetoric, in other words, was just a cover for internal repression. There have even been calls in Israel to support Assad, because his Alawite background could make him the sole remaining partner for the Jewish state in the entire region, partly because that cult—according to this particular commentator—incorporates some Jewish, as well as Christian, rituals.[23] Be that as it may, if the Sunni Islamists take control, anti-Israel rhetoric could at long last be matched by political, and possibly military, action. A Sunni-led regime aligned with Saudi Arabia would probably move Syria away from Iranian influence and patronage.

But as in Lebanon, where the Hariri dynasty is the Saudi proxy, there are no guarantees that the Saudis will call all the shots.

AFTER MONTHS OF BLIND SUPPORT, Iran offered its first public criticism of the Assad regime at the end of August 2011. In a statement that closely echoed the one issued simultaneously by Nasrallah in Lebanon, it called on the Syrian regime to listen to "some" of its people's demands and start to implement reforms. As with the Saudi move, human rights was not the motivation. Iran, it seems, woke up to how vulnerable its position was becoming. If Assad was overthrown, Tehran would lose to Saudi Arabia a crucial political ally that acts as its conduit for aid to Hezbollah and Hamas in the Gaza Strip. But there was another reason little understood in the West: Iran itself is a deeply fragmented country, split along regional and sectarian lines. Western commentators often point out how sectarian unrest in Syria could spill over into Lebanon, but the risk of its doing so is perhaps greater in Iran.[24]

Only roughly one-half of Iran's 70 million people are ethnic Persians. The rest are Azerbaijanis, Kurds, Arabs, Turkmen, Baluchis, and Lors. This unusual diversity makes Iran not so much a nation-state as a multinational empire dominated by Persians, much as the Saudi state is dominated by the Wahhabis who conquered its various territories in the 1920s and subsequently imposed their mores and religious beliefs on everyone else. Iran's ethnic minorities share a widespread sense of resentment, accusing the central Tehran government of discrimination and neglect. Tehran's highly centralized development strategy has inevitably resulted in a wide socioeconomic gap between the center and the periphery, together with an uneven distribution of power, socioeconomic resources, and sociocultural status. Fueled by these long-standing economic and cultural grievances, unrest among these large groups of ethnic minorities such as the Kurds and Turkmen has been increasing over the last decade.[25]

The neoconservatives have long viewed this ethnic tension in Iran as an opportunity for achieving their goal of bringing down the regime through clandestine funding for opposition groups and armed separatists, perhaps in conjunction with a bombing campaign against the country's nuclear facilities. This aspect of Iran's internal geopolitics is likely to come into play much more in the coming years, and the disintegration of Iran could prove one of the most dramatic consequences of the Arab Spring. Western policymakers historically have paid little attention to Iran's ethnic tinderbox, but by the mid-2000s they began taking a greater interest. According to exiled Iranian activists reportedly involved in a classified American research project, the U.S. Department of Defense started examining the depth and nature of ethnic grievances against the Islamic theocracy. The Pentagon was especially interested in whether Iran would be prone to a violent fragmentation along the same kinds of fault lines that are splitting Iraq and that helped to tear apart the Soviet Union with the collapse of Communism. American intelligence experts infer that this investigation could indicate the early stages of contingency planning for a ground assault on Iran or be an attempt to evaluate the implications of the unrest in Iranian border regions for American soldiers stationed in Iraq and for Iranian infiltration into Iraq.[26]

The investigative journalist Seymour M. Hersh claimed that the Americans already had troops on the ground in Iran,[27] although it is quite possible that Hersh, in this instance as in many others, may have been played by his Washington sources as part of their psychological warfare campaign against Iran. A conservative think tank in Washington meanwhile held a conference on Iran that reportedly triggered uproar among exiled opposition groups, and especially among Persian nationalists. The conference was entitled "Another Case for Federalism?" although its chairman denied it sought to foment separatism.[28]

When President Ahmadinejad first came to power in 2005, he made an election pledge that he and his ministerial team would visit all of Iran's thirty provinces within their first year in office to settle long-standing local problems, many of them related to ethnicity or religion. Naturally, like most election pledges made by politicians everywhere, it came to nothing, and by the end of his first year in office, he had visited only about half of them. In fact, a number had effectively become off-limits for him because of escalating ethnic and sectarian tensions. Indeed, Iran was at the time experiencing some of the worst ethnic violence in its modern history.[29] The Iranian clerical regime does not publicly deny the hazards of the country's multiethnic nature, but official public statements from senior regime figures tend to blame "outside interference" for any signs of unrest. The day after the government closed a state-run Iran newspaper for publishing a riot-inducing cartoon likening ethnic Azeris to cockroaches,[30] Ahmadinejad predictably resorted to the tried-and-tested strategy of accusing America and its allies of hatching plots to provoke ethnic tensions that would destabilize his country. "The United States and its allies should know that they will not be able to provoke divisions and differences, through desperate attempts, among the dear Iranian nation," Ahmadinejad said in a speech broadcast live on state-run television.[31] Similarly, Britain, widely reviled by the Iranian government and public alike as a perpetual meddler in internal Iranian affairs, was repeatedly blamed for violence in Khuzestan, Iran's oil-rich southwestern region bordering Iraq and populated by Iranian Arabs who have close historical as well as tribal ties to Iraqi Arabs across the border.[32] Behind the scenes, however, the Iranian government does discuss the root causes of ethnic disturbances a little more soberly. The Islamic Majlis Center for Research, an Iranian government think tank, has warned in one report that the country will face even more serious internal unrest unless the government addresses the needs of its ethnic minorities. It pinpointed two key challenges: unemployment among young people across all ethnicities and regions, which it said would end up fanning the flames of resentment toward Tehran, and poverty among non-Persian ethnic groups in the border areas, who are historically vulnerable to outside manipulation.[33] Azeris, Kurds, Arabs, Turkmen, and Baluchis: all these groups share ties with people in neighboring Azerbaijan, Iraq, Turkmenistan, Afghanistan, and Pakistan, which are either traditionally hostile to the ayatollahs or contain American and other Western troops. This internal unrest is, to reiterate, a clear threat to the Iranian government's control of its land and population, and nowhere is it truer than in the southwestern province of Khuzestan, which, with its huge resources of oil, gas, and water, is the nerve center of Iran's economy.

In 2011, as if to confirm Tehran's worst fears, the Arab Spring swept through Khuzestan. An opposition group there, the Ahwaz Liberation Organization, said "thousands" of protesting Ahvaz residents had been killed by the Revolutionary Guards. How much of that claim was based on reality, and how much on the propaganda wars, is anyone's guess. What is especially noteworthy, though, is the vehicle through which they made their announcement: the Saudi-owned pan-Arab newspaper *Asharq Al-Awsat*.[34] Khuzestan's vast plains are punctuated by the flaring of gas at dozens of oil drilling rigs, which provide Tehran with about 80 percent of its revenue from crude oil production. Unrest here among ethnic Arabs, home to many of Iran's 2 million Arabs, presents Tehran with an especially serious domestic threat because, despite its vast natural resources, the province ranks among Iran's poorest and least developed. Again, this shows Iran as a mirror image of Saudi Arabia, where the Shia minority is concentrated in precisely the area that produces the most oil, the largely impoverished Eastern Province, and therefore bears the brunt of the central government's pigheaded maltreatment. Sun-battered and windswept, Khuzestan is one of those corners of the world, like parts of sub-Saharan Africa or Afghanistan, that are subject to seemingly endless calamities. It was relentlessly bombed by Iraq during the 1980–88 Iran-Iraq War, when its main cities were decimated. As late as the mid-2000s, the capital Ahvaz lacked a decent hotel, and when I arrived there in 2006 for a weeklong stay, I was greeted by the stench of an open sewer near the main hospital. That, too, mirrors the Saudi malaise, where despite unimaginable oil revenues many of the streets to this day flow, not with milk and honey, but with liquid shit.

In Ahvaz, drug addiction was also a major problem. In the evenings, the riverbanks were teeming with groups of addicts discussing their progress, or lack thereof, toward rehabilitation, under the supervision of social workers. Yet before the war with Iraq, the province had been among Iran's most developed. When Iraq invaded in 1980, hoping to take advantage of the postrevolution chaos to seize the oil fields, Saddam portrayed himself as the liberator of the Khuzestan Arabs. Although many Arabs in the border towns openly backed Iraq, the majority elsewhere did not, perhaps because they were Shia who saw their fellow Shia in Iraq persecuted by Saddam's own secular Baathist regime. Local ethnic Arabs complained to me that, as a result of their divided loyalties during the Iran-Iraq War, they were viewed more than ever by Tehran as a potential fifth column, and so suffered under a quasi-official policy of discrimination. In one Arab village about three miles from Ahvaz, to which an Arabic-language taxi driver took me while my government-appointed minder was sleeping in the hotel, pipelines ran right among ramshackle homes to carry oil from the nearby drilling rigs to refineries near the Persian Gulf. "We don't have any freedom here," one local young man, who worked as an engineer at a drilling rig, told me. "We are standing on all of the country's wealth, and yet we get no benefit from it."[35] A group of men from his village had quickly gathered in his courtyard to share with me their grievances. They said that Farsi was the only language taught in their village school even though all the students were Arabs and that no Arabic-language newspapers were allowed to be published in the province. They also claimed to suffer much higher levels of unemployment and poverty than local Persians. "The government says we are traitors," one of them announced, and added that he, like most members of his family, was unemployed. "But we are Iranians," he wanted to emphasize. "It's the government in Tehran that's treacherous, because it refuses us equal rights."

I was the only Western journalist who had visited that province for years. At the time of my visit, there was no evidence of anti-Western sentiment, and there was a general excitement among those to whom I talked about stories of a greater Western interest in their plight. They had the impression that I was on some kind of reconnaissance mission for the British government. So hated was the regime in Tehran that one man told me, as though I should pass on the information to my British spymasters, that he would welcome British forces as liberators, should they decide to expand their invasion from Iraq—he knew that the British troops in Iraq were mainly concentrated just across the border in the southern Iraqi city of Basra. Even so, all were scathing about the invasion of Iraq itself. "What use is democracy and freedom if there is no security?" was one typical comment. Just before I arrived, a series of bombings in Khuzestan had killed twenty-one people in the wake of antigovernment riots, and the central government was swift to implicate about fifty Arabs. At least twenty were reported killed, and hundreds were injured in the riots themselves. Amnesty International said that security forces then summarily executed many of those arrested.[36] The scale of the riots would probably have escaped foreign attention, except for a video shot of the riots by a crew the Al-Jazeera television news channel managed to get into Khuzestan, as a result of which Al-Jazeera was subsequently barred from reporting from the province.[37] What had immediately infuriated rioters was a leaked letter attributed to former Iranian vice president, Muhammad Ali Abtahi, that disclosed plans to expel Arabs from the province and replace them with ethnic Persians. Ahmadinejad himself was forced to cancel three trips to Ahvaz at the last minute. The official reason given each time was bad weather, but the real cause was likely security threats: one of the worst bombings, in which eight people were killed, took place just hours before the president was to address a public rally. Two ethnic Arab men found guilty of bombing a bank in January 2006, killing six people, were then, in the inimitable Iranian tradition of popular justice, publicly hanged from a crane in Ahvaz. The day before they were hanged, three other Iranian Arabs were reportedly executed in a local prison; and opposition groups overseas said that more local Arabs were facing death. More mysteriously, major oil pipelines supplying crude oil to the Abadan refinery on the shore of the Persian Gulf caught fire a few days after the hangings, probably because of sabotage.[38] Other pipelines in Khuzestan were bombed and supply temporarily interrupted, and Tehran announced it had foiled an attempt to bomb the Abadan refinery with five Katyusha rockets.[39] Certain Ahvazi Arab tribal leaders were said to have been armed by the regime to help guard oil installations. As a result, they had indepth knowledge of the pipeline infrastructure, according to the British Ahwazi Friendship Society, which lobbies on behalf of the ethnic Arabs.[40] It would have taken very little to persuade them to share their knowledge and turn their weaponry to other ends. Amid continuing international sanctions over its alleged nuclear arms program, Tehran could ill afford a serious disruption to the oil supply in Ahvaz.

The Abadan refinery represents about 30 percent of Iran's total refining capacity, a fact not lost on Al-Qaeda, which at the time of the bombings was reported to be shifting the focus of its campaign in the wider Persian Gulf to sabotaging oil facilities.[41] Iranian officials continue to this day to blame violence in Khuzestan on exiled separatist groups operating from Iraq, and they are furious that Canada, Britain, and America allow opposition groups based there to operate freely. At least sixty Arabic-language opposition radio and satellite television stations are beamed into the province from around the globe. "These groups incite terrorist acts and inflame the situation by spreading false reports," Khuzestan's deputy governor, Mohsen Farokhnejad, said when I met him. "Why do these Western governments allow them to do this when they claim to be fighting terrorism?" Although not confirmed, the Movement of Ahwaz, another very popular group operating from Canada and running a widely watched satellite TV station, does, to some, seem at times to verge on advocating a popular armed uprising.

THERE ARE CLEARLY MANY LOCAL ARABS in Khuzestan who still hear that call, making the region Iran's Achilles heel. If Syria disintegrates into sectarian and regional violence, it is here, in the heart of the country's oil industry, that the Iranian regime will face the most serious seditionist repercussions. In such a scenario, the West would be tempted to foment discord. But the exiles were right: it would indeed be a grave mistake for the West to attempt to involve itself in Iran's ethnic tensions for short-term political and military gain. Based on historical precedent, this would likely unleash a wave of Iranian nationalism and a massive backlash against any minority group seen as colluding with outsiders. Even the right-wing, Arab-Iranian exile Amir Taheri, otherwise a fervent backer of the neoconservatives' interventionist policies in the Middle East, has warned that fanning the flames of ethnic and sectarian resentment is not difficult, and a Yugoslavia-like breakup scenario might hasten the demise of the Islamic republic, but to do so would also "unleash much darker forces of nationalism and religious zealotry that could plunge the entire region into years, even decades, of bloody crises."[42] In any case, with the possible exception of the Kurds, none of Iran's ethnic groups is now seeking to secede from the Iranian state. The violence in remote regions such as Khuzestan clearly has ethnic components, but the far greater causes of the poverty and unemployment that vex members of those ethnic groups are government corruption, inefficiency, and a general sense of lawlessness, which all Iranians, including Persians, must confront. Rather than seeking to explicitly manipulate ethnic tensions in a futile request to change Iran's regime on the back of the Arab Spring, Washington should tread very softly indeed. For the consequences of an ethnic implosion in Iran would make the religious, tribal, and regional warfare elsewhere in the region look like a high school prom.

FIVE

LESSONS FROM SOUTHEAST ASIA

IN JULY 2011 TENS OF THOUSANDS OF MALAYSIANS DEFIED POURING rain to gather in the country's capital, Kuala Lumpur, to advocate for freer and fairer elections. The local and Western press were quick to describe the event as marking the beginning of the country's own version of the Arab Spring, and there were indeed striking parallels. For a start, the protesters were fed up with the decades-old domination of the ruling United Malays National Organization (UMNO) and the crony economy that had grown up around it. They came, as the saying goes, from all walks of life, and from all ethnic groups, in this religiously diverse country of 28 million (about 60 percent of whom are Muslims). Moreover, they had gathered under the banner of greater freedom and a more equitable distribution of the profits from the country's burgeoning economy. Again, as in the Middle East, the state's reaction was as brutal as it was disproportionate. After liberally firing tear gas into the crowds, battalions of armored riot police closed in on the unarmed protestors. No fewer than 1,600 of them were bundled off to jail. The demonstrations, like the rain, then petered out.

Among the victims of the police crackdown was Anwar Ibrahim, often simply described as Malaysia's "opposition leader." When he was pictured in a hospital bed, attached to a drip and oxygen tank, he was still wearing the yellow shirt of Bersih ("Clean"), the pro-democracy coalition movement under whose banner the protests had been organized. Anwar had suffered bruises to the head and legs, he later revealed, and also announced on Twitter that he had to undergo a CT scan. "I'm fine," he finally told his followers. "Just feeling a little dizzy."

It was not the first time that Anwar had had occasion to display his government-inflicted injuries to the world. Photographs of the bruises he sustained in police custody in 1999, after being arrested at the behest of the ruling UNMO, were also splashed across the front pages of newspapers. For the better part of the early millennium, indeed, he sported a neck brace. His ordeal greatly endeared him even to such beady-eyed international policemen as Paul Wolfowitz, who saw in him the voice of Malaysian democracy, a label that his most recent misfortune only served to strengthen. But what had Anwar done to provoke such loathing from the forces of Malaysian law and order—than which, it should be said, few more powerful forces exist in the country?

The short answer is that trying to co-opt Anwar was the biggest mistake of Malaysia's long-term autocratic prime minister, Dr. Mahathir Mohamad, who had been a humble provincial physician until fate propelled him to greater heights. An ardent Malay nationalist, Mahathir was nonetheless, before everything else, a modernizer, and very much a man of law and order. With a country doctor's brisk pragmatism, he brooked, above all, no nonsense. A Malay and a Muslim, Mahathir believed that Malay Muslims ought to pull themselves together, shake off their postimperial lassitude, overcome the advantages gained in colonial times by the smart, hardworking, efficient Chinese minority, and set the country on the path to modernity. He therefore instituted sweeping affirmative action for Malays and embraced Islam only as one facet—though an important facet—of ethnic Malay identity. He was thus assured the majority vote in election after relatively free-and-fair election.

By all accounts, Mahathir's program was a spectacular success. Malaysia under his decades of rule swiftly became one of the leading "tiger" economies of Southeast Asia. Even Western luminaries like Margaret Thatcher ardently admired him for his aggressive support for business and education, coupled with suppression of political freedoms. It will not do to sneer at the last qualifier. Malaysia, like Tunisia, has excellent roads, fine education and health systems, and world-class airports. In the Petronas Twin Towers, it also has one of the tallest buildings in the world. People go about their business ("business" being the operative word) by and large unmolested by the state security apparatus. And following the 1997 Asian economic crisis, Mahathir famously defied the International Monetary Fund and, all predictions to the contrary, by doing so set the country back on track faster than any of its neighbors who had fallen victim to the crunch.

However, despite all the affirmative action, which essentially meant that most public-sector jobs went to what Mahathir insisted on calling the Malay "race," those who most fervently embraced the business opportunities his policies opened up remained the Chinese. The cheap labor on which the tiger economy relied were, moreover, still ethnic Malays or, increasingly, immigrant laborers from Indonesia and elsewhere. At the same time, Mahathir's policies fostered a moneyed Malay elite, who now control an estimated 55 to 60 percent of the economy.[1] No matter how hard Mahathir tried, in other words, the grievances of the Malay masses would not go away. Rather like neighboring Malay Singaporeans, they refused, to put it frankly, to pull themselves up by their bootstraps. It follows that a significant minority saw the glitzy malls rise up all around them but could not afford to shop there and became impatient for other solutions. Increasingly, they were drawn to fundamentalist Islam through the insidious influence of the Wahhabis and the Muslim Brotherhood.

IN THE 1980S, THE LEADING EMISSARY of the Muslim Brotherhood in Malaysia was the oft-beaten opposition leader Anwar Ibrahim. He is the founder and head of the Malaysian Islamic Youth Movement, and one of the founders of the International Institute for Islamic Thought (a Muslim Brotherhood front[2]). If Malaysia is the nearest equivalent Southeast Asia has to Tunisia, in the sense that autocratic rule has combined with impressive economic growth and a historically liberal and open society that embraced diversity as a key to its strength, in certain ways Anwar could be considered its version of Tunisia's Islamist leader Rachid Ghannouchi. Like Ben Ali of Tunisia, Mahathir should at least be given credit for recognizing the enemy so early on, though perhaps an element of self-fulfilling prophecy is also at play. In any case, Mahathir evidently hoped to neutralize the Islamists, as the Tunisian regime had; but he tried to co-opt them instead of imprisoning and exiling them. In 1981, as soon as he became prime minister, he began to woo Anwar, and in the face of some consternation among his followers, Anwar was eventually persuaded to join Mahathir's UMNO, the ruling party, the next year.

Mahathir is a sour, brisk, nondescript little man, whereas Anwar has the burning eyes and grand gestures of a demagogue. Still, in many ways Anwar was Mahathir's evil twin. Where Mahathir was nationalist, Anwar was ultranationalist. As a university student, Anwar had defaced English-language signs; and one of his proudest achievements, during his tenure as education minister, was to rename the local language from "bahasa Malay" to "bahasa Melayu"—in other words, from Malay to even-more-Malay Malay. Where Mahathir was a conservative Muslim, from sheer confidence in his own rectitude, Anwar was, and remains, an avowed Islamist, of the notoriously humble variety.

For the longest time, Mahathir and Anwar danced a perfect minuet around each other, all the while keeping the hardline Muslim and working-class Malay vote focused on the UMNO. This, though, inevitably required concessions on the part of Mahathir. In 1993, he duly made Anwar his deputy prime minister and publicly anointed him as his successor. The next year Sunni Islam was declared the official religion of Malaysia, from which all other forms of Islam deviate. Power, though, failed to compromise Anwar, and he remained as hardline as he had been back in 1968. If anything, the concessions only emboldened him. On top of that, it might be said of Anwar that he knew nothing of gratitude. For example, he pushed through some governance regulations that went directly against Mahathir's anything goes business deregulation policies. Mahathir realized that he would never tame his protégé, and eventually he lost patience. In 1998, Mahathir fired him, citing allegations of corruption and sodomy—homosexuality being illegal in the country.

There followed the beatings in the police cells already mentioned, which resulted in Anwar displaying his neck brace, like Our Saviour's stigmata, for years to come. There was a mock trial, during which a semen-stained mattress was preposterously dragged into court as evidence of Anwar's alleged deviation. That a sly fox like Mahathir should have fumbled the matter so badly testifies to the enormous frustration he must have felt. But even at the densest of the fog over his brain, Mahathir had the sense to try and hit his Islamist nemesis where it hurt most: in the taboo-infested groin. By then, though, it was too late. Anwar was duly convicted and sentenced to fifteen years in jail for sodomy at first instance (officially the case is still ongoing), though no one in his right mind believed the charges, and fewer still seemed to care one way or the other. The result, though, was that a hero of Islamist democracy was born. Mahathir, it must be conceded, tried his darnedest to regain the Islamist high ground—declaring himself a "fundamentalist," sprouting anti-Zionist statements that often veered toward more straightforward anti-Semitism, suddenly claiming Malaysia was already an Islamic state, and (ever the racist) accusing the "Anglo-Saxon" race at the height of the Iraq war of being born warmongers.[3] But nearing eighty years of age, Mahathir was a spent force. In 2003, he finally resigned his UMNO leadership in a spectacle of fake tears and pleas to reconsider the decision that has made him the laughingstock of the world on YouTube.

The biggest beneficiary of all this nonsense was the hardline Islamist opposition. The most extreme of the Islamist political outfits, the Malaysian Islamic Party (PAS), took advantage of the political chaos and steadily gained ground by sticking to what it holds dear and true: implementing Islamic law. Now it rules four of Malaysia's northern states: Kelantan, Penang, Selangor, and Kedah. On the federal level, the PAS has been trying to moderate its hardline image to draw more Malay voters away from UMNO, but in the states where it is in power, it has instituted the usual Islamist policies. Kelantan, where it has ruled the longest, for instance, bizarrely has segregated supermarket checkout queues, which is unheard-of even in Saudi Arabia. The same state has introduced a premodern "Islamic currency" of fat gold coins for bigger purchases. Women must wear headscarves to work—always a trivial matter, until the Islamists are in a position to enforce it. And nightclubs are banned, leading to a flood of Malays escaping for the weekend to the brothels and karaoke clubs across the border in southern Thailand. All four states, moreover, have vowed to crack down hard on that most terrifying menace to civilization: Valentine's Day.

In short, the PAS is an exact equivalent of the Islamist parties of the Middle East, which present themselves as democrats, and do indeed embrace the democratic process so long as it suits them, while all the time steadily and intractably getting on with their real agenda of Islamizing society from below by instituting their fundamentalist, minority vision of society on the majority from any point where they can find leverage. Nationwide, the Islamists have whipped up such a wave of Islamist hysteria in this once liberal country that women are caned in public for drinking alcohol, "effeminate" schoolboys thought to show traits of homosexuality are sent away to heterocamps to have it drilled out of them, a Saudi-style religious police prowls the streets arresting unrelated couples out for a stroll, and—no, this is not a joke—the whole country has been obsessed for the last few years with the question of whether Christians should be able to use the word Allah for God.[4] In the federal parliament, meanwhile, the undisputed leader of the Islamist opposition bloc is now that hero of democracy: Anwar Ibrahim. It came as no surprise to anyone that, during the rainy July 2011 democracy protests in Kuala Lumpur, three main slogans were heard from the crowds: "Reformasi," "Long live the people," and "Allahu abkar."[5]

Malaysia, then, offers an example of what happens when so-called moderate Islamists are appeased by the liberal elite. They provide cover for their more extremist allies to transform society, so it eventually looks like a crude imitation of Saudi Arabia (a totalitarian country, incidentally, whose gross human rights abuses Islamists elsewhere of whatever stripe never dare to criticize). The parallel, as I have said, is most strikingly with Tunisia. However, the examples offered by Indonesia, the world's most populous Muslim country, and southern Thailand, with its Muslim majority, also serve as portents of what happens to historically liberal, diverse, and democratic Muslim societies once Saudi/Wahhabi influence begins to gain leeway. Saudi Arabia, we should remember (as we turn to Indonesia and southern Thailand), in addition to flooding postrevolutionary Egypt with cash and hijacking the political process in Bahrain, Yemen, and Syria, is also pushing for Jordan and Morocco to join the Gulf Cooperation Council, giving rise to the nightmare scenario of a sort of Greater Wahhabi Kingdom from the borders of Israel to the Atlantic. Just as worryingly, Saudi Arabia is trying to persuade Indonesia and Malaysia to join an alliance against its (and Washington's) archenemy, Iran.[6] When it comes to the latter effort, Riyadh's Wahhabi preachers have for a long time been laying the groundwork.

HIDDEN A FEW KILOMETERS DOWN a remote country lane in the heart of Thailand's troubled deep south sits the multimillion-dollar campus of Yala Islamic College. With more than a dozen Arab teachers from across the Middle East and a seemingly endless flow of funds, mainly from Saudi Arabia, the college, with its all-reflective surfaces and eerily anodyne atmosphere, make a person feel as if he had suddenly been transported to one of Riyadh's centers of higher education. The thousands of local students attending the college dress in Arabic clothes, and they are taught a strict interpretation of Islamic law in the Arabic language. The receptionist introduces himself, in perfect classical Arabic, as a graduate of Al-Azhar University in Cairo. And the president, Dr. Ismail Lutfi, was—as he would proudly tell me—a graduate of a hardline Wahhabi institution, namely Riyadh's Imam Muhammad bin Saud Islamic University. In a 2003 list of Saudi Arabia's most wanted Islamist terrorists, more than half were graduates of that venerable institution.

Dr. Lutfi, a gracious, crisply starched middle-aged gentleman who told me he is against violence, has thousands of followers installed in key Islamic posts throughout the south. But the Thai south's largely unregistered pondoks (Islamic schools)—which offer religious education, a regular curriculum, and training in Arabic and the local Yawi dialect—are nonetheless recognized by the Thai government as breeding grounds for radical separatists. A number of the Muslim separatists killed on April 28, 2004—when more than a hundred Muslims were gunned down on their motorcycles by soldiers acting on a tip about a planned series of raids on army posts across the south—taught at or were students in these local Islamic schools.

Religious schools have been springing up all over Southeast Asia since the late 1990s. Everywhere in this region, men and women are dressed after Saudi fashion—the men in short white thobes, caps, and loose head covering, the women in all-over black sacks and often even black gloves. Yet, historically, hard-line Wahhabi doctrine, and desert dress understood as an outward manifestation of religious purity, were anathema to the tolerant traditions and ethnic and cultural diversity of Southeast Asia, where Islam was a relatively late addition to the local spectrum of beliefs and has traditionally been syncretic. Local Muslim "saints" were worshipped—or perhaps it is better to say venerated—alongside the spirits of the forest. Buddhists, Muslims, and Confucians in cities and villages tended to join in the celebrations of each other's holidays, not least because in a community of a few hundred souls it would have been rude to do otherwise. Those familiar with Egypt's popular Sufi culture of saint worship, and the historic warm relations the country's Muslims and Christians have enjoyed, will notice the parallels.

Indonesian, Malay, and Southern Thai Muslims developed their own costume, which for more pious women included a colorful headscarf that covers the hair and is closed under the chin, while the men wore caps and attractive "tailed" turbans fashioned from white or colorful cloth. Headscarves were by no means worn by all Muslim women, whether in cities or villages, and rarely if at all around the house or in the immediate rural neighborhood (even in traditionally pious communities). In areas where the belief systems overlap, it was not uncommon to find people praying in the mosque, but also consulting witch doctors about certain problems, or making offerings to the tree spirits just in case.

Syncretic Islam, then, means the adaptation of the religion to practical circumstances, local traditions, and entrenched ways of life. In truth, all Islam is syncretic in that sense. The form believed to have existed in the time of the Prophet Mohammed, and the forms that exist in the Arabian heartland today, are in turn only adaptations of "heathen"—that is to say pre-Islamic and tribal— traditions and mores. In Mecca before Islam, people used to run naked around the Kaaba in a form of pilgrimage, while the Kaaba itself was already the center of the local religion and contained dozens of idols (which the Prophet famously smashed to pieces). The fashions that the extremists like to describe as "Islamic dress" are actually Bedouin costume. Even the segregation of the sexes, without which Islamists believe the entire world will imminently perish, has its roots in the social code of desert bandits, who regarded women as chattel and used to carry them off together with other movable spoils in the short time available during a raid. So it was wiser to keep women out of sight. The veiling of women, too, about which the Quran is ambiguous, has its grounding in tribal culture, which places a great deal of emphasis on a man's honor and pride; and it is therefore easier to blame women for constituting an irresistible temptation than for men to acknowledge their failure to resist it. It is for reasons like these that academics quite properly describe the spread of fundamentalist Islam in the wider Muslim world not as "Islamization" but "Arabization." The latter term not only more accurately reflects what is taking place, but also usefully identifies the source of the trouble: the Arabian Peninsula.

In Southeast Asia, the Wahhabization process began in the 1960s, when the ideas of the Muslim Brotherhood were the great intellectual fashion among Muslim students, much as Marxism and Maoism were the intellectual fashion among students in the West. At the same time, the Saudis began to sponsor a great number of educational activities among clerics in Southeast Asia, even among quite moderate ones. The result was that the Hanbali school of Islamic jurisprudence—the most literal and extreme, which is prevalent in Saudi Arabia—found a foothold there. In the 1980s and 90s, the Saudis, and to a lesser extent the Kuwaitis, moved on to flooding the regional book market with cheap Wahhabi tracts, often of an anti-Semitic, anti-Shia, anti-Christian, anti-everything bent, as is the nature of the sect's learned literature, which, alas, is, by and large, devoid of any positive and humane message.[7]

The Islamists were helped in this effort to promote extremism by two factors. For one thing, Indonesia and Thailand were what is called "labor-exporting" countries. In other words, there was a constant stream of menial workers who went to the Persian Gulf and were exposed to Wahhabi fundamentalism, which they were often persuaded by noisy, browbeating preachers must be the true Islam; and then they returned home to spread the word. As we have seen, this is also primarily how Wahhabism managed to gain a foothold in Egypt in the 1970s. But unlike the Egyptians, Southeast Asian Muslims by and large speak no Arabic, meaning even many who have memorized the entire Quran in the original language may have only the most nebulous idea of what any of it actually means. They are, therefore, dependent on the glosses provided by their preachers, who in turn may be no great linguists and rely on the free commentaries the Saudis—in their international manifestations as the World Assembly of Muslim Youth and the International Islamic Relief Organisation—so generously distribute among the benighted.

An additional, related problem is that practically nobody, even in Arabic-speaking countries, understands the complex language of the Quran (reading it is like asking someone who never even reads contemporary English literature to suddenly read Chaucer), so it follows that even educated Southeast Asians who do speak Arabic need help from the so-called scholars. What does it mean, for example, when the Sura Al-Noor instructs women to cover in public their *juyubihinna,* "except what ordinarily appear thereof"? The word *juyubihinna* seems to be a solecism, like *mobled* in Shakespeare. Some learned people suggest it means "ornaments," others "breasts." How much of whatever it may be can be said to appear "ordinarily"? It is really anybody's guess, but for most ordinary people it stands to reason that the local cleric's guess must be better than their own, since it is, after all, his sole function to relieve them of constant bellyaching about the small print of their religion so they can get on with the infinitely more interesting business of living their lives.

The battle for hearts and minds is very much between entrenched local traditions on the one hand and on the other people with the determination and money to meddle with them. That invariably means fanatics or, if such a distinction can be drawn, the Wahhabis. This is the story everywhere in the wider Muslim world. Students go to the Middle East on generous scholarships and study Salafi or Wahhabi doctrine, and they learn there that jabbering on at top volume about martyrs and violent jihad is a highly effective way of whipping up religious fervor. In the home country, hardline religious schools spring up, like the one I visited in Thailand, and spread their obsession with ritual, code, dress, and other apparent trivia. Above all, they spread their obsessive-compulsive cult of purity, their absolutist adherence to a never-never true and original faith shorn of all "innovations"—such as decency, humanity, and common sense. In turn, the students go forth into their hometowns and villages and, clothed in the aura of their superior education and Bedouin fancy dress, hector and bully their peers into accepting these absolute truths of which they now find themselves in possession, in the process eradicating the "wrongness" that has taken centuries to build up.

WHEN I VISITED THE SOUTHERNMOST THAI PROVINCES in 2004 to write a series of articles on one of the most violent Muslim insurgencies the world has ever known, more than 160 Thai Muslim students were enrolled in Islamic institutions in Saudi Arabia and 1,500 were studying in Egypt.[8] Thailand's then deputy prime minister, Thamarak Isarangura na Ayuthaya, said his government believed there were military training sites in Saudi Arabia, Pakistan, and Egypt, where Thai Muslim separatists were trained to execute terror attacks back at home. But the government was then only just beginning to concede that it was facing a complex Islamist threat. There were signs that the terrorist group Jemaah Islamiyah, the regional Al-Qaeda franchise, was making recruits to its quest to establish a pan-Southeast Asian Islamic state from southern Thailand through Malaysia and Singapore and across Indonesia into the southern Philippines. Numerous regional leaders from Jemaah Islamiyah, Al-Qaeda, and the Free Aceh Movement had spent time in southern Thailand after the September 11 attacks. Independent estimates put Jemaah Islamiyah membership in southern Thailand alone at the time as high as 10,000, and the Thai military said at the time it was hunting down at least 5,000 armed separatists. Al-Qaeda's operational leader in Southeast Asia, Riduan Isamuddin, known as Hanbali, was no stranger to southern Thailand either before he was arrested north of Bangkok. According to Eric Teo Chu Cheow of the Singapore Institute of International Affairs, Jemaah Islamiyah members met twice in southern Thailand to plan the 2002 Bali bomb blasts and possibly other bomb attacks in Indonesia. Muslims in southern Thailand could have been discreetly plugged into the Jemaah Islamiyah network, he told me, and reportedly had close links to the two Muslim rebel groups in the southern Philippines, the Moro Islamic Liberation Front and the more deadly Abu Sayyaf group. Saudi Arabia's International Islamic Relief Organization (IIRO) is the largest donor to Islamic causes in southern Thailand. Hardly any educational or religious project had been untouched by the IIRO, which is part of the Wahhabi-funded Muslim World League. After September 11, the U.S. Treasury froze IIRO funds in America because of its links to Al-Qaeda.

It was clear to me after some weeks travelling through the southern Thai provinces that the situation there was much worse than Bangkok was willing to admit. The ethnic Thai Buddhist minority in the south was feeling increasingly besieged and circulating pamphlets (I was handed one) that detailed local Muslim extremism. In their view, it posed an unprecedented threat both to their religion and the state. One senior Thai government official in the Muslim-majority state of Pattani, clearly shaken by the recent events, told me he was aware of the first signs of "ethnic cleansing" (his words) in Narathiwat, one of the three Muslim-majority provinces, adding that some Thai Buddhist families had been told to leave under the threat of violence. Three Buddhist temples were attacked during the month I visited. Since then, the newspapers have relegated to their inside pages the day's, or week's, account of the slaughter in the south, almost invariably involving the barbaric beheading of lone rubber-tappers cycling to work at dawn, when the sap flows most freely—a thankless, poorly paid job that these often elderly victims nonetheless undertake to eke out a living for themselves and their families. Sometimes these easy, innocent targets are Thai Buddhists, sometimes they are Malay Muslims, and such is the heroism of the jihadis of southern Thailand rising up against their oppressor in the name of Allah.

A substantial number of radicalized Thai Muslims had fought with the Taliban against the Soviet occupation in the 1980s, and when they returned, they became teachers in the local Islamic schools. Yet the upsurge in violence was proving difficult to understand and control for the Thai government, because it came after Bangkok had effectively dismantled its intelligence apparatus in the area and scaled down its military presence, thinking it had all but crushed the separatist movement in the late 1990s—in hindsight, these older separatists seem a positively amiable bunch, and they were later to try and mediate in the standoff, but by then they had lost all their credibility among the young hardliners. A retired Thai general admitted to me that neither the military nor the police had a clue what was going on in the south. In the absence of crucial intelligence information, then Thai prime minister Thaksin Shinawatra—ever one to try and seek the most cursory quick fix—took refuge in routinely dismissing the jihadis as "crazy" and "bad boys." In fact, the Thai government's response under Thaksin made matters significantly worse. Under the allegedly corrupt billionaire prime minister's rule, two massacres of Muslims occurred in 2004. It is my understanding that while Thaksin is not responsible for these massacres, they did happen under his rule. In the first incident, mentioned above, soldiers followed a group of Muslim separatists who had sought refuge in the historically significant Krue Sae mosque and riddled 32 of them with bullets; they were later found in possession of nothing more than knives and a single gun.[9] In the second, the arrest of six suspected separatists sparked a demonstration by hundreds of locals in the town of Tak Bai. When some threw rocks and attempted to storm the police station, the army moved in with teargas and guns and "kettled" the protestors. They were stripped of their shirts and had their hands bound behind their backs before they were beaten, kicked, and stacked six deep like meat on trucks for transport to a military camp in Pattani, which for some reason took up to seven hours. Some eighty-five died of suffocation, heatstroke, or the consequences of beatings.[10] There is no evidence to suggest that Thaksin knew about or was in any way involved in the massacres.

It was a "show of force" that, as anyone could have predicted, backfired spectacularly. But that Thaksin will ever be prosecuted for his financial crimes seems increasingly unlikely now that his sister has become the first officially remote-controlled puppet prime minister of Thailand—"Thaksin thinks," was her slogan, "Pheu Thai [the current name of his much-renamed party] acts"—while her billionaire brother sits pretty in self-imposed exile in Dubai, or Montenegro, or Paris, until he is amnestied and has given back the money he stole from the Thai nation. The Muslims of southern Thailand could perhaps be forgiven for thinking that justice only awaits in the next world.

THAI MUSLIMS HAD LONG COMPLAINED of discrimination in jobs and education, along with the economic neglect of the south, and this had provided fodder for various separatist movements since the provinces—once part of the Muslim kingdom of Pattani—were annexed by Thailand in 1902. If an inordinate number of teachers, for instance, were targeted in the ethnic cleansing campaigns, it was partly because the dunderheaded central government, to enforce its cultural hegemony, made sure that they were ethnic Thai Buddhists. Local resentments, which the Islamists exploited by linking them to the wider Islamic struggle, became more intense. There was an alleged "hidden hand" in the violence by military and police, each vying with the other (and local separatists, who frequently double as criminals) for control of arms- and drug-smuggling rings—a situation in some ways reminiscent of the occupied Palestinian territories. Battalions of "rangers," who were essentially paramilitary thugs, were set up to patrol the villages. And there were almost continuous reports of false arrests and torture as the army reacted the only way soldiers know how: with jackboot and gun. The human rights lawyer Somchai Neelapaijit, who had defended a number of prominent Muslims, "disappeared" in Bangkok one night after being stopped by police and has not been heard from since.[11]

The impact of perceived American and Israeli attacks on the Muslim *umma* in the form of invasions of Muslim-majority countries in the wake of September 11 was also immense. Surveys showed that among Muslims in Thailand and throughout Southeast Asia, the invasion of Iraq, pictures from Guantanamo Bay, and tighter American visa regulations for Muslim visitors had severely tarnished America's reputation, and this had a radicalizing effect. In the Thai south and among Southeast Asian Muslims in general, there was a great deal of swaddling and beard growing among Muslim families, initially as a sort of political statement of solidarity against the besieged Muslim community rather than as a manifestation of religious fervor, but it inevitably played into the Islamists' hands.

Yet not all Thai Muslims were backing these developments. Vairoj Phiphitpakdee, a Muslim but not ethnic Malay member of Parliament for Pattani, said Muslims are mistaken to believe that Islam is just about adopting Arab customs. "They're taken to the Middle East and they're brainwashed," he told me. He was right, and wrong. Perhaps it would be more accurate to say that the Middle East comes to them and hitches a ride—like a parasite on a dog—on their grievances, their educational disadvantages, and their overheated nationalist feelings. The remarkable thing is that Islamism has found no great resonance in the adjacent provinces of Southern Thailand where Muslims are not the majority but still make up a substantial minority. In Krabi, for instance, where local officials may be ethnic Thais, business owners ethnic Chinese, and fishermen and artisans Muslims, the communities continue to live together with relatively little friction. Fully veiled women are a tiny minority; the sexes mingle freely; foreigners are invited to partake of feasts in Muslim settlements; and at least the children can take part in the more colorful festivals of other groups, like the popular water-throwing games of the Thai New Year, even if their parents may not put on any celebrations themselves. Meanwhile, in Bangkok, where Muslims tend to live in small villages amid the urban sprawl that are slightly (but only slightly) better than slums, fully veiled women also remain a rarity, and if a man is decked out in full Bedouin caboodle, he is usually more likely to be some forlorn Westerner who has washed ashore there and seen the light, rather than a madrassa-trained Thai.

What is interesting, in other words, is that these people are not much better off than their coreligionists in the south. Thai Buddhists generally look down on Muslims and suspect them of all manner of perversions, and they are by and large significantly poorer than their non-Muslim neighbors. The Muslims in Bangkok are not ethnic Malays but ethnic Thais, and the Islamist bug has not bitten them. This suggests that Islamism needs a distinct identity or a homogenous environment to latch on to: if everyone in the village, and the next village, is Muslim and they largely share the same grievances—if Muslims constitute at least some kind of local majority, even if they are the minority in the greater setup—then it can find a foothold. The simplistic nature of Islamism means that it thrives on victim narratives and clearly identifiable enemies. When there is no such simple, immediate outside threat against which sentiment can be rallied, and when peaceful coexistence is self-evidently in people's day-to-day interest, it finds it much less easy to gain traction.

Sadly, in the Middle East, with its long tribal and sectarian memories, the preferred Islamist narratives come ready-made (pitting for instance a corrupt secular elite against the hardworking, pious poor, or the rightly guided Muslim majority against deviant Christians), and leaves the population with no robust defenses against the ways in which extremists are able to exploit their situation.

IN INDONESIA, THE ISLAMISTS WERE UP AGAINST a seemingly insurmountable obstacle. Upon independence in 1945, the future president Sukarno had devised an official state philosophy named Pancasila that deftly embraced chauvinist and nationalist sentiment, religious feeling, and modern hunger for social justice, equality, and democracy. The name comes from the Sanskrit for five (*panca*) and principles, precepts, or cornerstones (*sila*), and thus in itself alludes to the deep Hindu-Buddhist past of the Indonesian islands. They are:

1. Belief in the one and only God
2. Just and civilized humanity
3. The unity of Indonesia
4. Democracy guided by the inner wisdom in the unanimity arising out of deliberations amongst representatives
5. Social justice for all the people of Indonesia

In formulating the first principle, the secular Indonesian founding fathers were careful to mediate between the representatives of the Muslim majority, who wanted the term "Allah," and the representatives of other religions, and instead used the more neutral Bahasa word "Tuhan" for "God." Again, this had the advantage of rooting the philosophy in a specifically Indonesian past, however legendary, rather than tying it too closely to Islam.[12] And while the term still seems to exclude polytheistic religions, it nonetheless represented, for most, an acceptable compromise, because they saw in the other principles an Indonesian form of living together that they felt able to reconcile with their religion. From the point of view of guaranteeing political rights, indeed, item 4 is the more controversial tenet, because Sukarno was swift to decide that democracy needed quite a lot of guiding by his own inner wisdom, and the last free elections until the overthrow of his successor and nemesis Suharto were held in 1955.[13]

For the longest time, nonetheless, this emphasis on Indonesian-ness kept the country relatively resistant to the influence of fundamentalist Islam, especially since Sukarno's own regime was quietly hostile to the religion, which it rightly saw as a threat to its modernizing aims.[14] But when Suharto overthrew Sukarno in 1967 and began to institute his New Order policy, a centralized, militarized dictatorship with hefty backing from a United States obsessed with stemming the threat of Communism in Asia, he rather went overboard. Suharto insisted on "indigenizing" Pancasila, claiming that the five principles were entirely rooted in Indonesian traditions, by which he meant the traditions of his home island of Java. This had the effect of alienating other parts of the country, where the ethnic resentments that Sukarno had sought to neutralize were never far from the surface. In turn, this prompted Suharto to rule with an ever heavier hand. He stifled democratic opposition, with the result that mosques became more important as places where people could express their political feelings, and as Muslims retreated behind the walls of their mosques and homes, so did other religions, which deepened divisions.[15]

By the time Suharto was finally thrown out after 32 years in power, the system, as under any long-reigning dictator, had become deeply corrupt, and the whole concept of secular government and Indonesian unity so discredited, that it became difficult to imagine what unifying principle other than Islam could hold the country together. On top of that came September 11 and the American invasions of Afghanistan and Iraq, which radicalized Muslims around the world. Since 2003, dozens of local governments in Indonesia have instituted Islamic bylaws, mostly in matters of family law, but also introducing curfews for unaccompanied women.[16]

Besides its tradition of tolerance, Indonesia seems to have an equal and opposite tradition of unruliness and mob violence, where it is not rare for one village to go on a revenge expedition to the neighboring village over a slice of cake, armed with sticks and stones, and wait for the first hapless fellow to come out so he can be subjected to a dose of tribal revenge. And for all that the people of these islands are proud Indonesians, they are even prouder—as Suharto's own example suggests—Javanese, Papuans, Acehnese, and so forth. They are often especially hostile to the ethnic Chinese, who play a scapegoat role somewhat similar to the Jews of Europe in the past, and the farther away they are from Jakarta and all it represents, the more likely they are to be stirred up in turn against the ethnic minorities in their midst.

Indonesian-ness, in short, is at the same time an extraordinarily powerful and an extraordinarily fragile thing, and the traditional tolerance and peace that lie over the jungle can very suddenly tip over into these isolated, volcanic eruptions of violence. It is unclear to what extent such incidents have increased—when press reports say something is on the increase, they usually only mean that the reporter has finally noticed it—but what is clear is that throughout the early years of the millennium, they increasingly took on a sectarian flavor. Fundamentalist hate preachers exploited this tendency toward mob violence, quite possibly making it worse, and Islamist groups like Hizb ut-Tahrir and, perhaps most egregiously, the Wahhabi thugs of Laskar Jihad[17] were at the forefront of raids, pogroms, and terrorist attacks. Public demonstrations, too, increasingly took on an Islamist flavor, partly because those were the only terms in which the normal complaints and calls for improvement of any voting public could be framed: if frustrated citizens had previously marched for better wages or housing, they were now demanding the stoning of adulterers.

There have been many incidents of Islamist mob violence, and there seems no end in sight—one Jakarta suburb now gets the worst of both worlds with constant clashes between Islamic and Christian fundamentalists.[18] But a few developments deserve looking at in more detail to illustrate the more insidious ways in which Islamism tends to poison the social fabric at the root and spread out through its branches—and also to show how a society steeped in many other things besides Islam can prove to some degree resilient enough to keep the infection at bay, even though this may in some ways feel like learning to live with diabetes.

THE PROVINCE OF ACEH IN NORTHERN SUMATRA had always prided itself on the special Islamic identity that set it apart from the rest of Indonesia. It proudly dubs itself the Veranda to Mecca, because it was here that Islam first entered Indonesia in the Middle Ages thanks to its geographical position as a bridgehead toward the Indian Ocean. There was an Islamic uprising in colonial times, and after Indonesian independence the province's relations with the central government remained, to say the least, uneasy. Already in 1959, Aceh was given the status of a special territory, but it continued to feel badly treated when foreign companies started exploiting its mineral resources and Suharto embarked on a campaign to industrialize the region. Human rights abuses by central government forces were widespread, and a long-running insurgency by the Free Aceh Movement (GAM) that began in the 1970s resurfaced with renewed vigor in the 1990s. For a while after Suharto's ouster, therefore, it was touch-and-go as to whether Aceh would break away from Indonesia altogether. But because Islam was historically so bound up with Acehnese regional identity, it occurred to Jakarta to throw it a kind of sop: in return for remaining part of Indonesia, the province could hold a plebiscite on whether it wished to institute Islamic law. In 2000, the Acehnese overwhelmingly decided in favor. However, this still did not end the insurgency; it took the devastating 2004 tsunami, which killed some 250,000 Acehnese, to trigger a peace process, and today the territory is largely ruled by former GAM fighters.

The institution of Islamic law did not bring an immediate revolution in the way people lived.[19] As their history shows, the Acehnese are above all else proud Acehnese and conservative Muslims because the religion represents much that is distinctive about the region. The capital city of Banda Aceh was never going to be a hotbed of vice, people were on the whole pious, and much of the culture centered on the family and the home. Since the Indonesian justice system was so corrupt as to be essentially nonexistent, perhaps there was hope that Islamic law offered a greater opportunity for equal justice for all (which is a point where the newly "liberated" Middle Eastern countries are particularly vulnerable). At the same time, the Acehnese were sure enough of their identity to consider themselves rather more civilized than the Arabs, so they were far less hysterical about such things as the subjugation of women than their would-be mentors in Arabia.

Still, Islamism is a one-way street. Before long, a religious police in Muslim-green fantasy uniforms were shining torches into the eyes of couples who sat too close together on the beaches, and wrestling with the crowds at pop concerts and ball games to keep boys and girls apart.[20] Though these official guardians of morality were perhaps clowns, they were clowns with a little power, and as I have said elsewhere, a little man with a little power is a dangerous beast. Calls began to grow for this or that transgression to be punished to the full extent of the barbaric laws. And there was a noticeable difference between the days before Islamic law, when people who wished to drink beer on the beach could do so openly, and the time since Islamic law, when they cannot. It is not, of course, unreasonable to argue that drinking beer on the beach is not the be-all and end-all of human existence, much as it could reasonably be argued that having to wear a headscarf is not the worst fate that could befall a woman. And indeed, as in Saudi Arabia, beer may still be drunk by those who know where to get it. Fundamentalism only ever deepens public hypocrisy, not public morality. The trouble is that there is a substantial minority in Aceh—a small middle class; students; non-Muslims—for whom Islamic law represents enough of a nuisance to prompt them to leave. The result is a brain drain, and the result of that is a hardening of fundamentalism, because not enough people smart enough to resist its creeping tyranny are left.

Because Islam is so tightly bound up with Acehnese exceptionalism, it has since the introduction of Islamic law become the territory's version of political correctness. There is no public forum where its tenets may be safely challenged. Aceh is never going to be in a position to divest itself of Islamic law without the implausible scenario of a violent revolution by secularists. Or to put it another way: Aceh has taken an impeccably democratic decision to divest itself of all future opportunities for democratic change. So what if the pious majority are comfortable having a bully around who tells them to behave as they would anyway, with a little ducking and diving to sidestep the law of the land? The question, rather, must be whether the setup offers sufficient space for those—albeit a small minority of some 40,000 non-Muslims[21] and a handful of educationally privileged people—who wish to live their lives differently, who consider it beneath them, as any citizen of San Francisco would, to duck and dive in order to go about their harmless pursuits. And the answer is that it does not.

Another interesting development is the way Islamism has infested the political system, again a warning for the Middle East. Perhaps the most striking example is the treatment of the minority Ahmadiyya sect, which finds its parallel in Egypt and Tunisia with the renewed persecution of Jews, Christians, and Sufis there. The Ahmadiyya are a slightly odd, peaceable outfit that take their name from a charismatic Indian windbag, called Mirza Gulam Ahmed, who claimed at the end of the nineteenth century to be divinely inspired, making the group a kind of Muslim version of the Mormons. Surprisingly successful from Lahore to Timbuktu, with membership in the tens of millions, the sect seems to have done little harm, and its beliefs look like a good-natured, nonsensical attempt to reconcile Islam not just with Christianity but with this and that from several other philosophies as well. From this ragbag, two tenets stand out. One is the somewhat fluid status of Mirza Gulam Ahmed—the promised Messiah, the Mahdi, and what else? "A prophet to unite mankind in the Latter Days."[22] How does that square with the Islamic creed, which says that Muhammad is Allah's prophet and represents the last word on the matter? The Ahmadiyya say Muhammad embodies "perfection" as far as being a prophet of Islam goes, but is that not a somewhat backhanded compliment? Is Mirza Gulam Ahmed not said to be *more* than a prophet? Worse, from the point of view of the Islamist, the Ahmadiyya believe that jihad is synonymous with *ijtihad* (interpretation) and means striving for personal perfection, a sort of doing the best you can, rather than the merciless slaughter of everyone who disagrees with you. And worst of all, the Ahmadiyya do proselytize, and they do make converts, in areas where the Islamists feel the only converts that ought to be made are theirs. It is easy to see how the group, for all their harmless hodgepodge of persuasions, should have been singled out for special condemnation by the hardliners.

There were mutterings in 2005 that the Ahmadiyya were becoming "more aggressive," and a recommendation was therefore lodged by some government agencies to ban the sect under Indonesia's age-old blasphemy laws.[23] A body called the Indonesian

Ulema Council (MUI) was tasked with deliberating on the sect's fate, with the result that three years later the Ministry of Religious Affairs and the Interior Ministry jointly issued a decree banning the Ahmadiyya from public worship.

"Members of the public are warned and ordered not to declare, suggest, or attempt to gain public support for an interpretation of a religion that is held in Indonesia or to conduct religious activities that resemble the religious activities of that religion which are deviant from the principal teachings of that religion," reads Article 1. Proposing to legislate what constitutes the principal teachings of a religion and what constitutes deviancy from it was bad enough and clearly demonstrates that the decree was nothing but a piece of meat thrown to the Islamist dogs—who themselves could, with some justification, be described as the worst deviants from a faith whose central teachings include that there shall be no compulsion in religion. What was more alarming was Article 4, which "warned and ordered" all members of the public "to protect and maintain harmonious religious life as well as peaceful and orderly community life by not conducting unlawful activities and/or actions against the followers, members, and leading members" of the Ahmadiyya[24]—a nudge and a wink if ever there was one. The ministries might as well have hung out a banner saying "Let there be pogroms," and sure enough, instead of settling the matter, mob violence against, and killings of, followers of the sect duly increased in the wake of the decree. In some ways the most striking effect of the decree, however, was to bring home how reactionary the MUI—a body set up by Suharto to co-opt and control the religious establishment—had become while nobody was looking,[25] and how abjectly willing the central government now was to oblige the Islamists by whatever means necessary, fair or foul, and to sacrifice the principles of tolerance and common sense to their grassroots tyranny.

THEN THERE IS THE EPIC SAGA of the terrorist leader Abu Bakar Bashir, who was the spiritual mastermind behind the 2002 Bali bombings (in which more than two hundred people were killed) and the bombing of the Marriott Hotel in Jakarta the following year (in which fourteen people died). Officially, he is the leader of the Indonesian Mujahideen Council and ran an extremist madrassa in Java that just happened to be the alma mater of an exceptional number of terrorists. But the CIA believes he also heads the Indonesian branch of Jemaah Islamiyah. Bashir claims JI does not exist, which may well be true, in the same way that Al-Qaeda only exists as a sort of concept and has come to mean any hard-line Sunni terrorist group. At the same time, however, he has quite openly hailed Osama bin Laden's terror campaign as "the struggle to uphold the true Islam."[26] Bucktoothed, mendacious, and evidently not quite right in the head—he has claimed the Bali explosives were only intended to maim, but were replaced by the Americans at the last minute with a "micro-nuclear bomb" to discredit the jihadis[27]—Bashir himself is not a very interesting figure. Like Rachid Ghannouchi of Tunisia, he spent a couple of decades in exile. Like Ghannouchi, he only came back after the secular regime that persecuted him had fallen, and again like Ghannouchi he admits nothing. But unlike Ghannouchi, he is openly in favor of terrorism, saying there is "no nobler life than to die as a martyr for jihad"[28]—though as such people often do, he has modestly left that distinction to others for 72 years and counting. If he is a poster boy for the Arabization of Indonesian Islam, it is partly because, like Bin Laden, he traces his ancestry back to Yemen.

What *is* interesting is that the Indonesian government treated Bashir with kid gloves all through the first decade of the millennium. When America put it to then-president Megawati Sukarnoputri—nation-founder Sukarno's daughter and no friend of radical Islam—that it would like Bashir "extraordinarily rendered" under the Bush administration's bizarre policy to abduct suspected terrorists and torture them in third countries, Magawati reportedly said: "I can't render someone like him. People will find out."[29] Prosecuted for involvement in the Marriott and Bali bombings, Bashir was cleared of the first charge and sentenced to a derisory thirty months in jail for "prior knowledge" of the Bali attack, but had even that conviction quashed on appeal and walked free. There were rumors that powerful figures in the military and politics were protecting him; he associated with one-time vice president Hamza Haz, whose interest in radical Islam seems to have been mainly that it would allow him to have several wives.[30] Not surprisingly, Bashir began to believe he was inviolable. If something as dismal and boring as an Islamist's career can be considered tragic, then it could perhaps be said that hubris proved Bashir's downfall. Had he decided to cut his losses after his release from jail, he could have ended his days as a respected elder statesman peacefully preaching hatred and poisoning the minds of the young. But no, the old man still had homicidal ambitions even if his mind was increasingly going, and he conceived the idea of setting up a terrorist training camp in Aceh. On the surface, that makes perfect sense, since the territory had voted overwhelmingly for Islamic law, and fundamentalist Islam was deeply ingrained in the social fabric. What better place than to recruit and train jihadis there? But as I have said, the Acehnese are first and foremost proud Acehnese, and they did not need a Javanese lunatic stirring up trouble in their midst with his alien ideas to radicalize them.

Also, the tide in Indonesia seemed finally to be turning. At the last elections in 2009, the Islamist parties for the first time in a decade lost ground, partly because many people simply had had enough of the constant violence and killing, and calls for violence and killing, the hectoring and bullying, the permanent Islamist revolution.[31] From a peak of 38 percent for all ten Islamist parties taken together, support declined to less than 30 percent. That is still an astonishing figure, but proof perhaps that when the Islamists are actually called upon to contribute to government, they are subject to the same rules as other politicians, and when Islam fails to deliver the promised answer, voters turn away. That, of course, is why in Egypt and Tunisia the Islamists are so reluctant to seek real political power. Significantly, the country's most hardline political outfit, the Prosperous Justice Party, now seems to have reached critical mass and is stuck at about 8 percent support.

It was amid this climate of cautiously resurging confidence, boosted by reports in the mainstream local and overseas press—which if there are enough of them can have the effect of creating the reality they seek to describe—that the political establishment finally realized it could "get" Bashir. It was not going to repeat the mistake of seeming to persecute a revered preacher for his religious views or suppressing a dissident voice with accusations of treason. This time, they were going to go strictly by the book and charge him simply with violating the criminal and terror laws, the most serious charge being soliciting donations intended for a paramilitary training camp.[32] This time the charge stuck, and in June 2011 Bashir was sentenced to fifteen years in jail.

AN AMUSING SIDESHOW TO THESE VERY SERIOUS developments was the Affair of the Handshake, which briefly brought Indonesia's minister of information and communication technology to wider international notice. Tifatul Sembiring is the leader of the Prosperous Justice Party, and his appointment to the post, given the small support his party enjoys, shows that the Islamist threat in Indonesia has by no means been banished. In his official capacity, Tifatul cannot only congratulate himself on his initiative to filter the Internet of "negative content" but also on bracing contributions on a number of subjects outside his ministerial remit, such as calls for Islamic law and total segregation of unrelated men and women in public at all times. He has, however, insisted that he is not a Wahhabi,[33] a public confession that in itself offers hope the Saudi preachers' influence in Indonesia may be waning. Enter Obama, on his 2011 mission to edify the Muslim world, and his radiant wife, Michelle. Who should pump the First Lady's celebrated upper extremity not with one but both hands, beaming from ear to ear? Tifatul Sembiring, of the fundamentalist leanings. Called to account, he claimed at first to have been "coerced" into physical contact with a woman evidently neither his sister nor his spouse. But the minister had reckoned without information and communication technology, and when a video of the handshake promptly surfaced on the Internet, he was forced into an embarrassing retreat.

Islamists false or true: "They are both the problem," the secular parliamentarian Budiman Sujatmiko sighed. "Don't ask me which is better or worse."[34] We need only glance at Tifatul's role model, Saudi Arabia, to better get a glimpse of the future that could still await Indonesia. In Saudi Arabia, a screaming panic seizes the clerics at the slightest sign of what they like to call "indifference to the veil"; women risk breaking the law merely by stepping outside of their homes unaccompanied by a male relative; extramarital sex is, in theory, punishable by public beheading or stoning. Yet 70 percent of marriages in the country are now reportedly of the "temporary" variety that can last as long as a few hours and are often a barely concealed cover for prostitution. And outright prostitution, while officially banned and harshly punished, is widespread in all strata of Saudi society, with the religious police even conducting regular raids on brothels in the holy cities of Mecca and Medina. All this would perhaps be tolerable if the result was that people could go about their private business undisturbed, so long as they did not make a song and dance out of their transgressions. That is how things played out historically, but not anymore. For a while in the early millennium, Jakarta had a reputation as the party capital of Southeast Asia. Obama chose the country for his latest address to the Muslim world precisely because of the fond memories he had of its traditional tolerance, which he experienced as a child in Jakarta. But the sight of men and women dressed incongruously in Bedouin tribal garb is now commonplace, and whether or not the Islamists are losing ground as a political force, as a social force they have in many places already won. The result is that for the ordinary Muslim, things are becoming as difficult as in the streets of Riyadh. The lies ordinary Muslims need to tell in public grow taller, and there is a constant need for random examples to be made of hapless violators, who may be punished today for what only yesterday seemed widely tolerated.

"WE WANT OUR FREEDOM SO THAT WE CAN FORM political parties in a pluralist civil society," a student member of Egypt's Muslim Brotherhood, and a professed moderate, told the BBC in March 2011. Remarkably, he then went on to cite Malaysia as an example of Muslim country he would like to see Egypt emulate. "You cannot judge us until you give us the chance," he continued. "We Islamists need a chance."[35] The lesson from Malaysia for the Middle East, and for this particular Islamist if he takes a moment to observe the reality, is blindingly clear: you cannot co-opt the Islamists, however democracy-loving may be some of their rank and file. Give them an inch, and they take the whole playing field and then change the rules of the game to make sure it is only they who ever get to win. Above all, you cannot beat the Islamists at the long game. When it comes to sheer endurance they will always have the edge. The very definition of moderation is knowing when to stop. What all the Islamists have in common is that they never let up for a second. To quibble with Islam, or, more precisely, with what the Islamists define as Islam, has become the equivalent of advocating that the age of consent be abolished in a full session of the U.S. Senate. Once the Islamists take charge, all arguments must be carefully couched in Islamic terms. Such support as secular movements once enjoyed go up—at least publicly—in smoke. In August 2011, Malaysian activist Norhayati Kaprawi, the director of a documentary about the new stricter women's dress codes in her country, said some women she interviewed had refused to show their faces in her film. They did so not on religious grounds, but because they feared reprisals. Malaysia is a country living in fear of the radical Islamists, she said. "If you don't follow the mainstream you will be lynched," she said, adding that people who hold more progressive or alternative views "don't dare to speak up in public."[36]

SIX

WHAT NEXT?

PRESIDENT GEORGE W. BUSH WAS RIGHT TO PUSH HIS "FREEDOM agenda" for the Middle East, crowed one neoconservative writer, Max Boot, as the Tunisian uprising shook the world in January 2011.[1] How different things looked back then to most outside observers, if not to me. Ben Ali had just fled Tunisia. The most modern and progressive country in the Arab world with the best-educated population looked set to transform itself into North Africa's version of Portugal. Mubarak was about to fall in Egypt. That country, too, has a rich and deep history of tolerance and pluralism and interfaith harmony. Mubarak would be driven from power as the result of one of the most popular revolutions in history, and the Islamists had shunned it. On Facebook and Twitter, youthful Middle Eastern voices, from Jordan to Algeria and Yemen, were demanding democracy and freedom—albeit in suspiciously idiomatic English. At play, we were told, was a kind of benign version of the domino theory. Liberal democracy would sweep unstoppably through the region. Once one dictator had fallen, surely the rest would topple in his wake.

From the outset, it was clear to me that Boot's dictum was wishful thinking. Already the Bush doctrine had made a vicious mockery of it. Iraq, since the American-led invasion, had descended into a lawless sectarian hell, and democracy had brought to power, with Nour Al-Maliki, a Tehran lackey determined to create a Shia theocracy in Iran's image. The democratic government of "liberated" Afghanistan had proved itself a corrupt bunch of clansmen. Its writ, a decade after that country's "liberation," barely ran beyond the capital, Kabul, and even that city could not, in any meaningful sense, be said to be under full control of the central government. From the ashes and slaughter had emerged a sole negotiating partner who offered Washington any hope of a more stable future and a safe exit from the mire: the Taliban, against whom America had gone to war in the first place.

No sooner had Ben Ali fled than thousands welcomed back Tunisia's exiled Islamist leader Rachid Ghannouchi. Before long, one Internet ban in Tunisia had been replaced with another, even broader one; women were being attacked for not wearing the veil; and zealots were prowling the streets seeking converts. And all this despite Ghannouchi himself calling for a more moderate Islamist society. In Egypt, Mubarak was ousted, and then churches were burned down, the shrines of moderate Sufi Muslims were smashed to pieces, and men with unkempt beards and fiery eyes assaulted women protestors and demanded an end to the sale of alcohol and the wearing of bikinis on the beach. In Syria, a wary secular regime was about to get busy bludgeoning the Islamists.

Saudi Arabia's "day of rage" was briskly preempted by a religious establishment that rallied as one behind the geriatric rulers and declared all demonstrations un-Islamic. The Saudi masses nodded sagely and stayed home. Washington meanwhile perfected its hypocritical policy in the region by looking the other way as those Saudis who did step out of line were dragged off to jail. In tiny neighboring Bahrain, Saudi tanks crushed the uprising, even as Obama was busy delivering one of his professorial lectures about democracy to the Muslim world. In Yemen, Al-Qaeda in the Arabia Peninsula took over whole towns in the name of the Arab Spring, while the Islamist Islah party hijacked the mass demonstrations in the same country.

To be sure, there were liberals among all these protestors. They were mostly young people who wanted greater freedoms, and they looked to the West—perhaps more to Europe rather than America—as a model for their future. Where else were they to look? There were also among them middle-aged intellectuals who believed the time had come for their lifelong dreams to become reality. But they were, it is now obvious, a tiny minority, who had neither the ruthless political skills nor the popular support they needed to triumph. The vast bulk of the protestors knew nothing of political ideology. They were brought into the streets, not by a burning desire for free and fair elections, but by the dire economic circumstances in which they lived. For that they blamed their corrupt regimes, Israel, and, yes, the West, too, as they had long been accustomed to doing. Even the liberals—and this point cannot be made forcefully enough—were deluding themselves when they sought in the West a solution to their home-grown problems. The supposedly stable Western democracies they took as their role model had taken centuries to grow out of the gradual, painful, and bloody retrenchment of religion, on a rich soil of wars, ethnic cleansing, genocide, and brutal experiments in political utopianism. The West's wealth and power had grown out of centuries of exploitation of poorer countries. As the global financial crisis of 2008 showed, the West relied on blind consumerism driven by fragile financial fictions and a black hole of derivatives and debt invented and maintained and exploited by a nexus of multinationals in cahoots with a global political elite increasingly unaccountable to the masses. After centuries, the Western democracies, then, were finally crumbling, just as the young liberals of the Middle East took to the streets hoping to make it all happen again in twenty-four hours. That is the great irony of the Arab Spring.

The Arab liberals also mostly overlooked that the current leader of the free world, though of a different color, was the same in every particular when it came to the Middle East as the previous leader of the free world. The bankers still dictated American fiscal policy. So long as "stability" was under threat anywhere in the world, these tireless defenders of freedom would cling to their alliances where they could, or otherwise form new alliances with the most reactionary, compliant, and corrupt partners they could install. In other words, the dreams of the Arab liberals were in the end themselves reactionary: they were founded on an idea of what their countries should have been had they been somewhere else entirely. Freedom and representative government were enormously attractive ideas, as they remain in the West, and just as Communism remained almost throughout the eighty dismal years of the Soviet Union. But now that they have failed to materialize, they look implausible in the Middle East, to the point of madness. In much of the region the liberals among the protestors would have done better to stay indoors and put their considerable resources instead into planning a swift journey into exile.

Interviewed amid the smoldering husks of the Arab Spring in August 2011, the astute Egyptian scholar, Samir Amin, noted that there were "certainly many risks, including, in the medium term, the risk that a reactionary, Islamist alternative may prevail." That, he conceded, was Washington's plan, "unfortunately backed by Europe as well, at least as far as Egypt is concerned." The plan, he explained, is to establish an alliance between the reactionary Egyptian military rulers and the Muslim Brotherhood, which is, moreover, an alliance supported by Washington's allies in the region, led by Saudi Arabia—supported even by Israel. So, will it succeed? It is possible that it will work in the medium term, but it won't provide any solution to the problems of the Egyptian people. So, the protest movement, the struggle, will continue and magnify.[2]

Amin's analysis of Obama's realpolitik is spot-on. He backed the Saudis in their invasion of Bahrain, backed Al-Qaeda-linked rebels in Libya, and backed the Saudi counterrevolution more generally throughout the region that relied on the support of the Muslim Brotherhood, its affiliates, and even more extremist Salafi groups from Tunisia to Egypt, Yemen to Syria. But in asking himself whether the liberals' push against this Washington-Riyadh counterrevolution will succeed, Amin starts to wander off into quite a different realm of analysis. No one knows what will happen in the Middle East in the long term. Maybe the Arabs will be the first to put a man on Mars. It is the medium term that matters, and, for all the optimism that still prevails, for those who care to look at the reality on the ground, it is obvious that the Islamists will triumph. Of course, as Amin also rightly points out, the Islamists do not offer a solution to the economic and social woes that brought the protestors into the streets. But they offer something seductive in the absence of meaningful solutions: a simple answer, *Islam is the solution.* The Islamists offer solace in the face of insurmountable problems, and the terrible price that the ordinary people of these countries will have to pay for that solace will only much more gradually become evident. As the Saudi and Iranian examples show, it is effectively impossible to get Islamist dictatorships out of power once they have consolidated themselves. Even Turkey, with its once unshakably secular political-military ruling class, is inching toward an Islamist electoral dictatorship. So long as the Islamists have the support of the vast pious hinterland, democracy plays into their hands, because the liberal, progressive, secular elite by definition makes up a much smaller portion of the electorate. All the Islamists need is enough buses to cart their faithful supporters to the polling booths.

An article in the weighty *Foreign Affairs* magazine in 2011 showed how effective the Islamists who will rule in the medium term have been in their overseas propaganda, deftly playing on Washington's addiction to geopolitical chess games. "There is no question," wrote Shadi Hamid of the ultrapragmatic Brookings Institution, "that democracy will make the region more unpredictable and some governments there less amenable to U.S. security interests." But fear not: "mainstream" Islamists like the Muslim Brotherhood in Egypt and Ennahda in Tunisia, Hamid assures us, "have strong pragmatic tendencies." They have shown that they are "willing to compromise their ideology" when faced with "difficult choices":

> To guide the new, rapidly evolving Middle East in a favorable direction, the United States should play to these instincts by entering into a strategic dialogue with the region's Islamist groups and parties. Through engagement, the United States can encourage these Islamists to respect key Western interests, including advancing the Arab-Israeli peace process, countering Iran, and combating terrorism. It will be better to develop such ties with opposition groups now, while the United States still has leverage, rather than later, after they are already in power.[3]

So the Islamists are coming to power, whether we like it or not, and we might as well back a winner. But what of the region's women, its Christians and Shia and ever-dwindling number of freethinking intellectuals, its ordinary moderate Muslim "folks," in Obamaian parlance, who do not particularly desire to live under a backward Wahhabi theocracy? They, it seems, can go to hell. American and Israeli "security interests" come first and are best served by a pact with the devil. If it really did serve such interests, that attitude, though deeply unethical, would at least be understandable from a purely pragmatic point of view.

The problem with the pragmatic argument, however, is that history has a habit of making mincemeat of it. The pragmatists backed one vicious South Vietnamese regime after another, but still lost the war and handed the region to China on a platter. The pragmatists backed the shah of Iran and the revolution in that country swept to power Ayatollah Khomeini. The shah fled at first to Egypt. Two years later his host Anwar Al-Sadat—who had given the shah refuge and was Washington's closest Arab ally after making peace with Israel—was assassinated by radical Islamists. In the 1980s, the Washington pragmatists armed Osama bin Laden and the Taliban. The pragmatists backed Al-Sadat's successor, Hosni Mubarak, another willing Western stooge, and in 2011 Egypt witnessed an action replay of the Iranian Revolution. Then there is Washington's eight-decade-long "engagement" with Saudi Arabia, the regional superpower—whence came Bin Laden and fifteen of the nineteen hijackers on September 11.

By backing the Islamist hijacking of the Arab Spring, Washington proves only that it has learned no lessons from the past, and the consequences for the future of the Middle East, not least where democracy and the fight against extremism are concerned, are dire. For the fact is that moderate Islamism is a myth. There are, to be sure, more than a billion moderate *Muslims*—people who pray five times a day or not, fast during Ramadan or not, perhaps entertain harmless superstitions about pork, the devil, or the conduct of the birds vis-à-vis the Kaaba, or indeed seek by painstaking study of the Quran and the hadith to reconcile the basic values of their religion with modern life and the discoveries of science. But *Islamism* is a political ideology that takes a literal, fundamentalist interpretation of the Quran as a master plan for society: Islamic law, the segregation of the sexes, the subjugation of women, the submission of the masses to clerical authority. You are either an Islamist or you are not, in the same way that you cannot be a little bit pregnant. As this book has shown, the only fundamental differences that exist between different brands of Islamism, whether Shia or Sunni, is in the speed and strategy with which they hope to achieve their aims, the actual system of governance used to implement them, and in what might broadly be termed foreign policy. Some Islamists wish to kill all infidels now and bring about a global caliphate after next Friday's prayers. Others are comfortable with domestic repression while sponsoring such influence on the world outside their national borders as the public coffers will permit, leaving the rest to Allah.

And it is here that the Islamists have been able to bamboozle Western policymakers with their pragmatic outlook. They have shown themselves flexible on such questions as America's invasions of other Arab countries or support for the right of the state of Israel to exist. They have mediated oil prices. They have bought vast arsenals of British and American weaponry. They have shaken hands with the unswaddled wives of American presidents. Or they have chosen a gradual approach to Islamizing their societies through existing institutions, gnawing a little bit off the constitution here, digging small tunnels under family law there, and generally cloaking themselves in the garb of responsible democrats. The Shia fundamentalist group Hezbollah, for instance, takes part in elections, provides adequate public services in southern Lebanon, and bans the sale of alcohol in the towns it controls. The Sunni fundamentalist group Hamas, also popularly elected, has formed an institutional government in the Gaza Strip and taken weapons out of the hands of a myriad rival militant factions, while using the relative ensuing calm to go about God's work of eradicating any trace of civil society and banning male hairdressers. In a way, Al-Qaeda and the Taliban were a godsend to these people. Simply by not being out-and-out terrorists, even the most vicious Islamist hardliners have been able to present themselves as staunchly moderate allies of democracy.

On top of all that, the liberal elite is discredited throughout the Middle East. It is seen as having feathered its nest and spouted rhetoric for decades without ever managing to ameliorate the behavior of the old secular regimes, far less to remove them from power and offer a viable political alternative. Moreover, where is the evidence, as the American classicist Bruce Thornton has asked, that the freedom demanded in the Middle East "is the freedom we believe in?" What if it means the freedom to be "a good Muslim living under sharia law," as we are told by both the Libyan National Transitional Council's draft constitution and the Cairo Declaration of Human Rights in Islam, whose Article 24 reads: "All the rights and freedoms stipulated in this Declaration are subject to the Islamic Sharia." This is not, Bruce points out, "to say that Muslims are incapable of liberal democracy, which is usually how reservations like those above are mischaracterized." It just means that for liberal democracy to develop in the Muslim Middle East, it will take much more than merely removing autocrats and holding elections. It will take a critical mass of Muslims themselves figuring out how to reconcile traditional Islam and sharia law with notions like universal human rights, tolerance for minorities, separation of church and state, and all the other bedrock principles of liberal democracy. Based on our own experience in Afghanistan and Iraq, the possibility of this sort of reconciliation seems remote.[4]

More to the point, Samir Amin is likewise right to say that Washington's interests in the region are above all those of its closest allies, Israel and Saudi Arabia. America will do everything in its power to further those interests, in the case of Israel for ideological reasons and in the case of Saudi Arabia to continue the flow of oil. That means, ironically, embracing the Wahhabi nexus in those countries where the Arab Spring has swept the old regimes aside. The Saudi-funded radical Islamists may in principle be opposed to Israel's existence. But while rich in symbolism, in the great geopolitical scheme of things, it makes little difference to anything what Tunisia does or does not do vis-à-vis Israel. Saudi Arabia's media and schools spew constant anti-Semitic venom, but the Al-Saud regime loathes Tehran much more than Tel Aviv. In Egypt, for all the anti-Israel rhetoric flying from every corner of the political spectrum, the military has made one thing clear: Come what may, the 1979 peace treaty between Egypt and Israel will not be scrapped. Democracy or no democracy, the Egyptian generals will continue to dictate foreign policy, and their priority is not what the masses want but securing the $1.4 billion in military aid they get from America annually. In fact, opinion polls continue to show that about half of Egyptians want the peace treaty to remain; and, as the country's postrevolutionary economy disintegrates, almost no Egyptian in his right mind wants all-out war against the Jewish state. If the Assad regime in Syria were to fall, the likeliest outcome would be a prolonged and bloody civil war. The last thing the Syrian army would be considering, either, as it battles to keep in power the regime it rules in partnership with, is a foreign war. If the Assad regime survives, on the other hand, it will be business as usual: lots of talk and absolutely no action. If anything, domestic unrest has made Israel policy an even lower priority for Damascus.

Washington itself was never likely to reconsider its staunch support for either Tel Aviv or Cairo's generals, still less so as unrest rocked the region and the containment of Iran remained its top priority. The drive to contain Iran was one reason Washington looked the other way when Saudi Arabia sent in the tanks to crush the uprising in Bahrain. Obama, as we have seen, did his Saudi friends the kindness of not mentioning them once in his much-trumpeted speech calling for greater democracy in the region, thereby implicitly giving the green light to the Al-Sauds' crackdown on dissent at home as well. And he continues to arm Saudi Arabia's ruling family. To contain Iran, Israel meanwhile sides with the Saudi regime—a country where the intelligentsia considers the Protocols of the Elders of Zion a genuine plan for a Greater Israel extending from the Euphrates to the Nile. For as long as this bizarre American-Israeli-Saudi political axis continues to hold tight, liberal democracy stands no chance of gaining a foothold anywhere in the region.

IF THERE IS TO BE ANY HOPE FOR LIBERAL DEMOCRACY in the Arab world, in short, change must first come to the West itself. And what hope is there of that? Well, there were some hints that just such a change might indeed be on the way, inspired no less than by the Arab Spring.

In May 2011, tens of thousands of young Spaniards gathered in one of Madrid's main square to express—as had their counterparts in Cairo's Tahrir Square—their frustration with growing unemployment and the austerity measures imposed by the Eurozone to prevent Spain from defaulting on its debt. "I'm here against the system, against everything, the banks, the government, the Popular Party, unemployment. You name it. Nothing works," one of the protestors declared.[5] Stated so baldly, the opposition sounds rather silly; but she had a point.

The Madrid protests, as in the Arab world, had been organized through social networking sites. Similar demonstrations took place in a number of Italian cities, in Greece, and even in Israel. In America, groups of "nonpartisan" protesters, again taking their cue from the Arab Spring, began under the banner Occupy Wall Street a protest in September 2011 because their country seemed destined to slide into another recession; the root cause was mainly the interplay between Obama's thralldom to the bankers on one hand and, on the other, the obstruction of progressive reforms by a religious fundamentalist opposition—the Tea Party Republicans—that appeared increasingly unhinged. "Special influence corrupts our political parties, our elections, and the institutions of government," the organizers of the protest said on their website. "Bought by hard and soft dollars, disloyal, incompetent, and wasteful special interests have usurped our nation's civil and military power, spawning a host of threats to liberty and our national security. We have had enough."[6]

Poor little bankrupt Britain, meanwhile, had its own moment of rage in August 2011. Wholly spontaneous, but without any political program, England saw mainly young people from disadvantaged backgrounds go on a looting rampage in the poorer parts of London and later of other cities, too. No slogans were chanted, no enemy identified, and pretty much the sole statement that was being made was that these people wanted home appliances. Yet in its own way the rampage was a rather more powerful political demonstration than the well-bred protests in the Mediterranean and America. Demonstrations are a democratic right within democracy, and often merely serve to affirm the validity of the system, whereas the English looters—who incidentally also coordinated their sprees by text messages—exposed the degree to which the system itself had become a sham. Consumption, they had been brought up to believe, was the highest good in a consumerist society. And, boy, did they loot to consume! The difference was that they did not see, given that the dice were hopelessly loaded against them, why they should pay for it. And even as their prime and foreign ministers spouted lofty platitudes about democracy while bombing Libya toward freedom, their own courts came crashing down on the rioters. Within days of the riots, England's notoriously slow justice system had processed hundreds of them and handed down scores of lengthy jail sentences for such egregious offenses as trespassing and stealing bottled water.[7] Only a few years earlier, during a visit by President George W. Bush to London, one million protestors—more than in almost any demonstrations of the Arab uprisings—had taken to the streets of London in peaceful opposition to the war in Iraq.

But no one resigned, no one fled the country, no one for one second thought to describe the event as an Anglo-Saxon Spring, and the illegal Iraq war went ahead to bomb that country back to the Middle Ages—with Britain's full diplomatic and military support.

Within the American political system, perhaps the most promising sign of change was Ron Paul's credible standing in presidential opinion polls. A libertarian and isolationist, Paul is against all American wars and occupations in the Middle East and elsewhere, which is to say he is against America's crude imperialist agenda. "I know the CIA has been involved in so many elections around the world, they pick and choose dictators. . . . I don't think there's any doubt they're very much involved in these revolutions going on in the Mediterranean, we're just trying to pick dictators," he has said.[8] Unlike Obama and British prime minister David Cameron, he at least understands that the old imperial powers can no longer afford their empires, and that their moral authority is so compromised worldwide that even heartfelt—read: deluded—appeals to freedom and democracy will inevitably ring hollow if at home you have the largest prison population in the world, if 15 percent of your population subsist on food stamps, if random police violence is a staple of the nightly news bulletins, if your Patriot Act further erodes year after year constitutionally enshrined civil liberties, and if your government is constantly teetering on the brink of insolvency.

Against Ron Paul's rising popularity, however, must be set the equally credible standing in the presidential polls of the other Republican frontrunners, who were so terrifyingly simplistic and shallow in their political outlook, especially when it came to global affairs, that they made George W. Bush of blessed memory look like a towering genius. Indeed, in the libertarian blogosphere, the shadings toward fascism, white supremacism, religious mania, and plain lunacy are so subtle as to make it very questionable whether even many of Paul's supporters support him for the right reasons, or whether they simply worship the libertarian label he has attached to himself. Obama's apologists in the American press meanwhile tend to present a picture of the president as a good man defeated by the system and by his own kindly intentions. That may seem implausible—a more likely view is that Obama is simply another inept stooge—but it suggests that his defenders deep down know the system to be stronger than any individual. They know, in other words, that all presidents are consumed by the presidency. In all likelihood, as president Ron Paul, in the highly unlikely event that the system allowed him to be elected in the first place, would turn out to be either just another carbon copy of the previous officeholders or, if not, would not still be around to complete a first term of office.

ONE EVENING IN THE SPRING OF 2011, I was sitting in a restaurant in the downtown district of Tunis, near where I was staying, when a man came in with his son. They timidly took a seat at one of the tables. They were evidently, judging by their dark skin, dress, and demeanor, up from the countryside for the day. For a long time they pored over the menu, occasionally asking questions of the waiter, until they ended up ordering more or less the standard fare of hummus, pita bread, and kebabs. To celebrate the occasion, the father treated himself to a beer. An old Marxist would have seen only injustice—in their timidity, in the fact that to them this run-of-the mill restaurant represented a kind of social pinnacle. But they were giving themselves a treat, and it occurred to me, as I watched them, that there are millions of people like them throughout the Arab world, and indeed throughout the world, who barely manage to negotiate the system to which they are accustomed. What right did anyone have to decide that they must "pay the price" for someone's pie-in-the-sky notion of liberal democracy? At least as things stood they knew, for example, what avenues to take if they had to submit any official paperwork, and they were able to enjoy such small freedoms as they had—a glass of beer after a day's work—without some straggly-bearded thug smashing them in the face for it. Of course, they ought to have better opportunities. Their old regime had failed to provide for them. But for all that, I feared for the future of these two innocents in the restaurant much more than I would have done if I had encountered them during Ben Ali's rule.

The Arab Spring has been a dismal failure. All indications are that what comes next will be significantly worse than what existed before, in Tunisia and everywhere else, and the traumatic events up to now have already caused untold havoc and violence and made the lives of innocent ordinary people even more miserable than they already were. Socially and economically, the Arab Spring has put back countries like Tunisia, Yemen, and Syria by decades.

In Britain, the masses were calling for the army to be deployed in the wake of three nights of rioting by a few hundred people, and the champions of democracy cowered in their little apartments, terrified. Yet all the while these same liberals were calling for more uprisings in the Arab world, more bravery from the protestors, more upheavals, more violence and chaos, anywhere except outside their own front door. In a sense, the liberals in the West are even more objectionable than the neoconservatives. Both, of course, are armchair generals, sipping on their claret and puffing on their cigars as they send thousands out of the trenches to certain death. As George Orwell famously said: "All the war-propaganda, all the screaming and lies and hatred, comes invariably from people who are not fighting." But at least the neoconservatives are honest: more power for America, more security for Israel, and bombs for anyone who stands in the way. The liberals, cowering under the banner of "humane interventionism," are no less imperialistic than before. As they sit in America and Britain repeating their democracy mantra, how hard they must have to work to blind themselves to the bankruptcy of their own political systems, to the extraordinary social decay and poverty in their own midst, to their economies on the precipice of collapse, to their bought-and-paid-for politicians, and to their increasingly timid and shallow corporate media. How self-deluded they must be to sing the praises of political systems, and even suggest them as models for others, when they have brought to power, through democratic elections, such scoundrels as George W. Bush, Tony Blair, Silvio Berlusconi, Vladimir Putin, and Nicolas Sarkozy. In the second quarter of 2011, the country in the European Union that showed the most promising economic growth, even of a still-poor 0.7 percent, was not Germany (which had 0.1), and not Brit-

ain (which had 0.2), but Belgium; and Belgium had had, for a year
and half, due to an unusual tangle in procedures, no government
at all. There were no harsh austerity measures in the wake of the
financial crisis, there was no wrangling about the budget; things
merely ticked over, undisturbed.[9] With the current crop of politicians in the Western democracies, it would seem that no government at all is better than being led by the elected geniuses.

The only long-term hope for progressive change in the Middle East—and that this represents some kind of hope reveals the
hopelessness of the situation—is for America to follow Britain's
route into utter irrelevance in the region. The objection to the
American empire is not that it is an empire per se, but that, arguably unlike that which was ruled by the British, it has for decades
been such an abysmally incompetent one, making matters worse
not only for people in the countries where it planted its two left
feet but for itself and its own people, too. We can meanwhile only
pray that the "peak oil" theory is right and Saudi Arabia will,
in the not-too-distant future, run out of it and thus return to its
pre-oil status as a dusty, irrelevant Bedouin backwater; and the
oil-rich ayatollahs in Iran will also lose all leverage outside their
own backyard. In the meantime, let us hope for no more violent,
dead-end revolutions. Monarchies, slowly but surely embracing
the constitutional model (as in Jordan and Morocco), would seem
to be the best that's on offer at the moment. And if it is good
enough for Britain, why not for the Arab world? These are not
especially brutal or militarized states, the Islamists there remain
in check, and their leaders are authoritarian but not madly repressive and enjoy widespread support—at least as much as is enjoyed

by the typical leader in the West. A certain amount of liberalism, moreover, is still at play in both countries, which is more than can be said for any of the others; and, compared to Britain and America, their economies are thriving, in the sense that their middle class is growing rather than being eviscerated. This might not be democracy as we know it and mostly love it, but it's the best kind the Arabs can hope for in the midterm. An ideal does not exist in reality anywhere and never will.

The best that ordinary, innocent people can hope for is to go about their daily business relatively undisturbed, without some foreigner coming in to bomb them to smithereens, or some bearded swine constantly bullying them about their religious duties and thus making their lives a nightmare, or someone else setting the little shop that feeds them on fire, someone who is propelled by God knows what moronic fervor.

NOTES

INTRODUCTION: AN ARAB SPRING?

1. See, for example, "The [Egyptian] Tyrant Must Go, but Beware What Comes Next," *Daily Mail* (U.K.), January 31, 2011, http://www.dailymail .co.uk/debate/article-1352090/EGYPT-RIOTS-Hosni-Mubarak-beware -comes-next.html; "Tunisia May be a Democratic Beacon, but Islamists Will Profit," *Daily Star* (Lebanon), February 1, 2011, http://www.daily star.com.lb/Opinion/Commentary/Feb/01/Tunisia-may-be-a-democratic -beacon-but-Islamists-will-profit.ashx#ixzz1Sp82U5CF; "Will Tunisians Rue Their Revolution?," *Jewish Forward,* February 2, 2011, http://www .forward.com/articles/135135/; and "Arabian Nightmare: Talk of an 'Arab Spring' for Democracy Is Dangerously Premature. An Islamist Takeover of the Middle East Is Just as Likely," *The Spectator* (U.K.), February 28, 2011, http://www.spectator.co.uk/essays/all/6725963/arabian-nightmare.thtml.

2. *Afrol News,* "Tunisia Tops Competitive Rank in Africa," June 17, 2009, http://www.afrol.com/articles/33565.

3. Agence France-Presse, "Islamists Urge National Reconciliation in Tunisia," July 18, 2011, http://www.google.com/hostednews/afp/article/ALeq M5hGT83MM5abyhd1ddTnyRYtUEH_8A?docId=CNG.8fb7d35155ba 255c40a5a227fc0d8daf.c1.

4. Mary Beth Sheridan, "Egyptians Say Economy Tops Their List of Concerns, not Democracy," *Washington Post,* June 4, 2011, http://www .washingtonpost.com/world/middle-east/egyptians-say-economy-tops -their-list-of-concerns-not-democracy/2011/06/04/AGUV31IH_story.html.

5. "After Their Revolutions for Peace, Crowd Violence Forces Football Match to Be Abandoned Between Egypt and Tunisia," *Daily Mail* (U.K.), April 3, 2011, http://www.dailymail.co.uk/news/article-1372844/After

-revolutions-peace-crowd-violence-forces-football-match-abandoned
-Egypt-Tunisia.html#ixzz1SpFMkSI9.

6. Tom Kington, "Refugees From Libya Attacked in Tunisian Desert," *The Guardian* (London), May 25, 2011, http://www.guardian.co.uk/world/2011/may/25/libya-refugees-gaddafi-regime-attacked.

7. Houda Trabelsi, "Tunisia Voter Registration Push Pays Off," *Magharebia.com,* August 18, 2011, http://www.magharebia.com/cocoon/awi/xhtml1/en_GB/features/awi/features/2011/08/18/feature-03.

8. Giuliana Sgrena, "Chaos Reigns in Tunisian Politics," Inter-Press Service, August 5, 2011, http://www.arabamericannews.com/news/index.php?mod=article&cat=ArabWorld&article=4566.

CHAPTER ONE: THE DEATH OF TUNISIA'S SECULARISM

1. Shashank Bengali, "Old Media Hands Remain in New Tunisia," *Miami Herald,* May 29, 2011, http://www.sentinelle-tunisie.com/medias/item/old-media-hands-remain-in-new-tunisia.

2. Alfred E. Montesquiou, "Tunisia Economy Thrives Amid Restrictive Politics," Associated Press, October 29, 2009, http://etaiwannews.com/etn/news_content.php?id=1094558&lang=eng_news&cate_img=35.jpg&cate_rss=news_Business.

3. Monia Ghanmi, "Porn Site Popularity Worries Tunisians," *magharabia.com,* April 27, 2011, http://www.magharebia.com/cocoon/awi/xhtml1/en_GB/features/awi/features/2011/04/27/feature-03.

4. Sayed Mahmoud, "Tunisian Bookstore Sees Demand Rise for Revolutionary and Islamist Publications," *Al-Ahram Online* (Egypt), July 19, 2011, http://english.ahram.org.eg/~/NewsContentP/18/16763/Books/Tunisian-bookstore-sees-demand-rise-for-revolution.aspx.

5. Agence France-Press, "Quarter of Tunisians Living in Poverty: Official," May 28, 2011, http://www.thefreelibrary.com/Quarter+of+Tunisians+living+in+poverty%3A+official-a01612467096.

6. John R. Bradley, *Behind the Veil of Vice: The Business and Culture of Sex in the Middle East* (New York: Palgrave Macmillan, 2010), p. 77.

7. Human Rights Watch, "Tunisia: Police Inaction Allowed Assault on Film Screening," June 30, 2011, http://www.hrw.org/fr/news/2011/06/30/tunisia-police-inaction-allowed-assault-film-screening.

8. Houda Trabelsi, "Salafist Ideology Threatens Tunisian Artists," *Magha rebia.com,* July 29, 2011, http://www.magharebia.com/cocoon/awi /xhtml1/en_GB/features/awi/features/2011/04/29/feature-04.

9. Barnabasaid, "Christians Flee as Islamist Influence Grows in Tunisia," June 6, 2011, http://barnabasfund.org/US/News/Archives/Christians-flee -as-Islamist-influence-grows-in-Tunisia.html.

10. *The Telegraph* (London), "Tunisian Fundamentalists Burn Down Broth- els," February 19, 2011, http://www.telegraph.co.uk/news/worldnews /africaandindianocean/tunisia/8335341/Tunisian-fundamentalists-burn -down-brothels.html.

11. Jamel Arfaoui, "Secularism Stirs Fresh Debate in Tunisia," *Magharebia .com,* March 16, 2011, http://www.magharebia.com/cocoon/awi/xhtml1 /en_GB/features/awi/features/2011/03/16/feature-03.

12. Bouazza Ben Bouazza, "Tunisia: Government, Islamist Party Condemn Grisly Slaying of Catholic Priest," Associated Press, February 19, 2009, http://www.startribune.com/templates/Print_This_Story?sid=1165305 88.

13. Ibid.

14. A video of the attack was posted on YouTube here: http://www.youtube .com/watch?v=hXr9Crc_RLc&feature=player_embedded.

15. Jennifer Lipman, "Arsonists Attack Tunisian Synagogue," *Jewish Chronicle* (U.K.), February 1, 2011, http://www.thejc.com/news/world-news/44533 /arsonists-attack-tunisian-synagogue.

16. The Associated Press, "Tunisian Police Fire Tear Gas on Islamist Protest," April 29, 2011, http://arabnews.com/middleeast/article377578.ece.

17. Hichem Borni, "Tunisian Protesters Demand Headscarves," United Press International, April 2, 2011, http://www.upi.com/News_Photos/News /Tunisian-protesters-demand-headscarves/4844/2/.

18. Meriem Zeghidi, "Is Tunisian Culture Under Threat From Is- lamists?," *France-24,* June 30, 2011, http://observers.france24.com /content/20110630-tunisia-culture-under-threat-islamists-attack-cinema -theatre-tunis.

19. Agence France-Press, "Tunisia's Internet Agency Agrees to Block Porn," June 14, 2011, http://www.google.com/hostednews/afp/article/ALeqM5h jgvniVzuE7YmFIresEi6lkwWQ5w?docId=CNG.b3569aafd06fe78f58be7 3c5faaa97a5.4a1.

20. Human Rights Watch, "Tunisia: Police Inaction Allowed Assault on Film Screening," June 30, 2011.

21. For a fuller discussion of Habib Bourguiba and his feminist legacy, see chap. 2, "Islamic Feminism," in Bradley, *Behind the Veil of Vice*.

22. Eric Pace, "Habib Bourguiba, Led Tunisia to Independence From France," *New York Times,* April 7, 2000, http://www.library.cornell.edu/colldev /mideast/bourgnyt.htm.

23. Ibid.

24. Gautam Naik, "Tunisia Wins Population Battle, and Others See a Policy Model," *Wall Street Journal,* August 8, 2003, http://online.wsj.com /article/0,SB106028926761045100-search,00.html?collection=wsjie%2F 30day&vql_string=tunisia%3Cin%3E%28article%2Dbody%29.

25. Ibid.

26. Quoted in Suha Sabbagh, *Arab Women: Between Defiance and Restraint* (New York: Olive Branch Press, 1998), p. 34. See also Richard H. Curtis, "Tunisia's Family Planning Success Underlies Its Economic Progress," *Washington Report on Middle East Affairs,* December 1999, http://www .wrmea.com/backissues/1196/9611072.htm.

27. Sabbagh, *Arab Women: Between Defiance and Restraint,* p. 34.

28. Montesquiou, "Tunisia Economy Thrives Amid Restrictive Politics," id =1094558&lang=eng_news&cate_img=35.jpg&cate_rss=news_Business.

29. Vincenzo Nigro, "Tunisia, il golpe italiano: 'Sì, scegliemmo Ben Alì,'" *La Repubblica* (Italy), October 11, 1999, http://www.repubblica.it/online /fatti/afri/nigro/nigro.html.

30. Elizabeth Day, "Fedia Hamdi's Slap Which Sparked a Revolution 'Didn't Happen,'" *The Guardian* (London), April 23, 2001, http://www.guardian .co.uk/world/2011/apr/23/fedia-hamdi-slap-revolution-tunisia.

31. Montesquiou, "Tunisia Economy Thrives Amid Restrictive Politics."

32. John Thorne, "Pre-Revolution Tunisians Were Growing Gloomier, Poll Shows," *The National* (Abu Dhabi), June 27, 2011, http: //www.thenational.ae/news/worldwide/africa/pre-revolution-tunisians -were-growing-gloomier-poll-shows.

33. Borzou Daragahi, "Neighbors in Tunisia Express Disgust Over Former First Lady's Family," *Los Angeles Times,* January, 2007, http://articles .latimes.com/2011/jan/17/world/la-fg-tunisia-villas-20110117.

34. *The National* (Abu Dhabi), "What WikiLeaks Revealed About Leila Ben Ali's Excesses in Tunisia," May 7, 2011, http://www.the

national.ae/news/worldwide/africa/what-wikileaks-revealed-about-leila
-ben-alis-excesses-in-tunisia.

35. David Gauthier-Villars, "How 'the Family' Controlled Tunisia," *Wall Street Journal,* June 20, 2011, http://online.wsj.com/article/SB10001424 0527487037524045761785236357181108.html.

36. Ibid.

37. Ibid.

38. Christopher Dickey, "A Dictator Dispatched," *Newsweek,* January 23, 2011, http://www.newsweek.com/2011/01/23/a-dictator-dispatched.html.

39. Colin Randall, "Tunisian Revolution Claims Victim in French Cabinet as Foreign Minister Quits," *The National* (Abu Dhabi), February 28, 2011, http://www.thenational.ae/news/worldwide/europe/tunisian-revolution -claims-victim-in-french-cabinet-as-foreign-minister-quits.

40. Gauthier-Villars, "How 'the Family' Controlled Tunisia."

41. David D. Kirkpatrick, "Behind Tunisia Unrest, Rage Over Wealth of Ruling Family," *New York Times,* January 13, 2011, http://www.nytimes .com/2011/01/14/world/africa/14tunisia.html?_r=2&ref=africa.

42. Associated Press, "Tunisian Ex-Leader: I Was 'Tricked' Into Leaving," June 21, 2001, http://www.cbsnews.com/stories/2011/06/21/ap/middleeast/main20 072872.shtml.

43. *France-24,* "Ben Ali Trial in Absentia a 'Charade,' Critics Say," Agence France-Presse, June 21, 2011, http://www.france24.com/en/20110621 -ben-ali-case-charade-tunisians-theft-embezzlement-trial-absentia -joke#.

44. Reuters, "Tunisia's Islamist Party Denies It's Behind Riots," July 19, 2011, http://www.jpost.com/Headlines/Article.aspx?id=230058.

45. This biographical sketch is drawn from Azzam S. Tamimi, *Rachid Ghan-nouchi: A Democrat Within Islamism* (Oxford: Oxford University Press, 2001).

46. Ibid., p. 6.

47. Ibid., p. 11.

48. Ibid., p. 19.

49. Ibid., p. 21.

50. Ibid., p. 26.

51. Martin Kramer, "A U.S. Visa for an Islamist Extremist?," *Washington Institute for Near East Studies,* June 21, 1994, http://www.martinkramer .org/sandbox/reader/archives/a-u-s-visa-for-rachid-ghannouchi/.

52. Tamimi, *Rachid Ghannouchi: A Democrat Within Islamism,* p. 96.

53. Ibid., p. 60.

54. Linda G. Jones, "Portrait of Rachid Al-Ghannoushi," *Middle East Report* (No. 153), July-August 1988.

55. Arthur Bright, "Islamist Leader Rachid Ghannouchi Returns to Tunisia. What's His Next Move?" *Christian Science Monitor,* January 30, 2001, http://www.csmonitor.com/World/terrorism-security/2011/0130/Islamist -leader-Rachid-Ghannouchi-returns-to-Tunisia.-What-s-his-next-move.

56. Associated Press, "Tunisian Islamist Leader: I'm No Khomeini," January 31, 2011, http://www.cbsnews.com/stories/2011/01/30/world/main73 00475.shtml.

57. Rachid Al-Ghannoushi and Linda G. Jones, "Deficiencies in the Islamic Movement," *Middle East Report Online* (July-August 1988).

58. "Tunisian Islamist Leader: I'm No Khomeini," The Associated Press, January 31, 2011.

59. Bassam Tibi, "Islamists Approach Europe: Turkey's Islamist Danger," *Middle East Forum,* Winter 2009, http://www.meforum.org/2047/islamists -approach-europe.

60. Guy Sorman, "Is Islam Compatible With Capitalism?: The Middle East's Future Depends on the Answer," *City Journal* (New York), Summer 2011, http://www.city-journal.org/2011/21_3_muslim-economy.html.

61. Nazanine Moshiri, "Interview with Rachid Ghannouchi," *Al-Jazeera English,* February 7, 2011, http://english.aljazeera.net/news/africa/2011/02 /2011233464273624.html.

62. Muqtedar Khan, "Islamists and the Problem of Double Discourse," *Huffington Post,* June, 30 2011, http://www.huffingtonpost.com/muqte dar-khan/islamists-and-the-problem_b_887314.html.

63. "The Rest of the Old Guard Must Go," *Spiegel Online* (Germany), January 24, 2011, http://www.spiegel.de/international/world/0,1518,741291,00 .html.

64. Rajaa Basley, "The Future of Al-Nahda in Tunisia," Carnegie Endowment for International Peace, April 20, 2011, http://carnegieendowment .org/2011/04/20/future-of-al-nahda-in-tunisia/ic.

65. Marc Lynch, "Tunisia's New Al-Nahda," *Foreign Policy,* June 29, 2011, http://lynch.foreignpolicy.com/posts/2011/06/29/tunisias_new_al_nahda; Giuliana Sgrena, "Islamic Force Rises in Tunisia," Inter-Press Service, July 31, 2011, http://www.ipsnews.net/news.asp?idnews=56694.

66. I was handed one of the flyers offering free instruction by a Tunisian friend.

67. Graham Usher, "The Reawakening of Nahda in Tunisia," *Middle East Research and Information Project,* April 30, 2011, http://www.merip.org /mero/mero043011.

68. *Spiegel Online* (Germany), "The Rest of the Old Guard Must Go."

69. Andrew Gilligan, "Tunisia: Birthplace of the Arab Spring Fears Islamist Insurgence," *The Telegraph* (London), May 28, 2011, http://www.telegraph .co.uk/news/worldnews/africaandindianocean/tunisia/8543674/Tunisia -Birthplace-of-the-Arab-Spring-fears-Islamist-insurgence.html.

70. Moshiri, "Interview with Rachid Ghannouchi."

71. Associated Press, "Tunisian Islamist Leader: I'm No Khomeini."

72. Tamimi, *Rachid Ghannouchi: A Democrat Within Islamism,* p. 87.

73. Ibid., p. 158.

74. *Herald Sun* (Australia), "Beer and Bikinis 'Not Under Threat' in Tunisia," July 21, 2011, http://www.heraldsun.com.au/news/breaking-news /beer-and-bikinis-not-under-threat-in-tunisia/story-e6frf7jx-12260954 92735.

75. Gilligan, "Tunisia: Birthplace of the Arab Spring Fears Islamist Insurgence."

76. Trabelsi, "Salafist Ideology Threatens Tunisian Artists."

77. Agence France-Presse, "Islamists Restore Order Amid Tunisia Violence," May 8, 2011, http://www.rawstory.com/rs/2011/05/08/islamists-restore -order-amid-tunisia-violence/.

78. *The Telegraph* (London), "Tunisia Extremists Firebomb Home of 'Blasphemous' TV Station Head," October 15, 2011, http://www.telegraph.co.uk /news/worldnews/africaandindianocean/tunisia/8828556/Tunisia -extremists-firebomb-home-of-blasphemous-TV-station-head.html.

79. Alexandra Sandels, "Islamist Protesters March in Tunisia, Riot Police Fire Tear Gas," *Los Angeles Times,* October 14, 2011, http://latimesblogs.la times.com/world_now/2011/10/tunisia-islamists-demonstration-nessma -tv-persepolis-elections-salafism.html.

CHAPTER TWO: EGYPT'S ISLAMIST FUTURE

1. For a detailed discussion of male prostitution in Luxor, see chap. 6, "Lost Dignity," in John R. Bradley, *Inside Egypt: The Land of the Pharaohs on the Brink of a Revolution* (New York: Palgrave Macmillan, 2008).

2. "Foreign Women Threaten Social Fabric of Luxor," *Al-Bawaba,* February 3, 2007, http://www.freerepublic.com/focus/f-chat/1793954/posts.

3. Hamza Hemdawi, "Reform of Egypt's Police Hits a Wall: The Police," Associated Press, September 18, 2011, http://www.google.com/hostednews/ap/article/ALeqM5ijDBVLcbcU29FKD89PjVmzdQx_Lw?docId=bb5fc4b396774295b00163de4930f06a.

4. Yaroslav Trofimov, "Egypt's Rulers Stoke Xenophobia," August 10, 2011, http://online.wsj.com/article/SB10001424053111904480904576498333697580942.html.

5. Hamza Hendawi, "Crime Wave Grips Egypt, Absence of Police Blamed," Associated Press, April 5, 2011, http://www.msnbc.msn.com/id/42427900/ns/world_news-mideast_n_africa/t/crime-wave-grips-egypt-absence-police-blamed/; Linda S. Heard, "Alexandrians Between Freedom and Anarchy," *Arab News* (Saudi Arabia), April 18, 2011, http://arabnews.com/opinion/columns/article364923.ece?service=print.

6. Hannah Allam, "Leadership Vacuum in Suez Illustrates Egypt's Instability," *McClatchy* Newspapers, September 13, 2011, http://www.mcclatchydc.com/2011/04/19/v-print/112444/leadership-vacuum-in-suez-illustrates.html.

7. Irfan Al-Alawi, "Egyptian Extremism Sees Salafis Attacking Sufi Mosques," *The Guardian* (London), April 11, 2011, http://www.guardian.co.uk/commentisfree/belief/2011/apr/11/salafis-attack-sufi-mosques.

8. Yasmine Fathi, "Protests Against Christian Governor Escalate, Salafists Dominate," *Al-Ahram Online* (Egypt), April 18, 2011, http://english.ahram.org.eg/NewsContent/1/64/10319/Egypt/Politics-/Protests-against-Christian-governor-escalate,-Sala.aspx.

9. *Al-Masry Al-Youm,* "Friday of Unity, People's Will," July 29, 2011, http://www.almasryalyoum.com/en/node/481565.

10. Yoroslav Trofimov, "Egyptians Turn Against Liberal Protesters," *Wall Street Journal,* August 2, 2011, http://online.wsj.com/article/SB10001424053111904292504576482563347097284.html.

11. Heba Hesham, "Nearly 90 Percent Trust SCAF to Lead Transitional Period, says Poll," *The Daily News* (Egypt), October 11, 2011, http://thedailynewsegypt.com/people/nearly-90-percent-trust-scaf-to-lead-transitional-period-says-poll.html.

12. Oren Kessler, "Egypt Bars Terror Group From Forming Political Party," *Jerusalem Post,* September 21, 2011, http://www.jpost.com/MiddleEast/Article.aspx?id=238793.

13. Patrick Martin, "Egypt Overturns Political Ban on Islamist Group with Terrorist Past," *Globe and Mail,* October 11, 2011, http://www.the globeandmail.com/news/world/africa-mideast/egypt-overturns-political -ban-on-islamist-group-with-terrorist-past/article2197311/.

14. See Bradley, *Inside Egypt,* p. 121.

15. Matt Bradley, "Emergency-Law Extension Worries Egyptian Activists," *Wall Street Journal,* September 14, 2011, http://online.wsj.com/article/SB 10001424053111903532804576568611926699764.html.

16. Mostafa Ali, "Military Council Fails to Defuse Mounting Tales of Torture in Egypt," *Al-Ahram Online* (Egypt), August 29, 2011, http://english .ahram.org.eg/NewsContent/1/64/19748/Egypt/Politics-/Military-council -fails-to-defuse-mounting-tales-of.aspx.

17. Samar Al-Atrush, "Mubarak 'Farce' Trial Stumbles," *Middle East Online,* September 6, 2011, http://www.middle-east-online.com/english/?id =47943.

18. *Deutsche Presse-Agentur,* "Rights Group: Less Freedom of Expression in Post-Mubarak Egypt," September 25, 2011, http://www .monstersandcritics.com/news/middleeast/news/article_1665001.php /Rights-group-Less-freedom-of-expression-in-post-Mubarak-Egypt.

19. Kristen Cook, "In Egypt's Tahrir Square, Women Attacked at Rally on International Women's Day," *Christian Science Monitor,* March 8, 2011, http://www.csmonitor.com/World/Middle-East/2011/0308/In-Egypt -s-Tahrir-Square-women-attacked-at-rally-on-International-Women-s -Day.

20. *BBC News Online,* "Egypt Women Protesters Forced to Take 'Virginity Tests'," March 24, 2011, http://www.bbc.co.uk/news/world-middle -east-12854391.

21. Pew Research Center, "Muslim Publics Divided on Hamas and Hezbollah," December 2, 2010, http://pewresearch.org/pubs/1814/muslim -public-opinion-hamas-hezbollah-al-qaeda-islam-role-in-politics -democracy?src=prc-latest&proj=peoplepress.

22. Dan Murphy, "Egypt Revolution Unfinished, Qaradawi tells Tahrir Masses," *Christian Science Monitor,* February 18, 2011, http://www.csmonitor .com/World/Middle-East/2011/0218/Egypt-revolution-unfinished -Qaradawi-tells-Tahrir-masses.

23. Bloomberg, "Egyptians Back Sharia Law, End of Israel Treaty, Poll Shows," April 26, 2011, http://www.arabianbusiness.com/egyptians-back -sharia-law-end-of-israel-treaty-poll-shows-396178.html.

24. Walid Phares, "Muslim Brotherhood Riding the Crest of Arab Spring," *Newsmax,* June 3, 2011, http://www.newsmax.com/WalidPhares/muslim brotherhood-arabspring-gadhafi/2011/06/03/id/398700.

25. *World Tribune,* "Young Activists See Muslim Brotherhood Alliance With Military Regime," March 28, 2011, http://www.worldtribune.com/world tribune/WTARC/2011/me_egypt0351_03_28.asp.

26. Sonia Farid, "Letter From Cairo: The One-Article Constitution," *Al-Arabiya Online* (Saudi Arabia), June 9, 2011, http://english.alarabiya.net /articles/2011/06/09/152625.html.

27. Phares, "Muslim Brotherhood Riding the Crest of Arab Spring."

28. Maggie Michael, "Egypt's Brotherhood Party Details Platform Akin to that of Iran," Associated Press, October 11, 2007, http://articles .boston.com/2007-10-11/news/29234166_1_egypt-s-brotherhood-draft -platform-parliament.

29. Investigative Project, "Egyptian Islamists Target Bikinis, Pyramids," September, 1, 2011, http://www.investigativeproject.org/3139/egyptian -islamists-target-bikinis-pyramids.

30. Khaled Abu Toameh, "The Muslim Brotherhood-Salafi Alliance: Will Egypt Become an Islamic Republic?" Hudson Institute, August 5, 2011, http://www.hudson-ny.org/2330/egypt-islamic-republic.

31. *Washington Times,* "Obama's Islamist Partners in Egypt," May 9, 2011, http://www.washingtontimes.com/news/2011/may/9/obamas-islamist -partners-in-egypt/; Maggie Michael, "Egypt's Brotherhood Party Details Platform Akin to that of Iran," Associated Press, October 11, 2007, http://articles.boston.com/2007-10-11/news/29234166_1_egypt-s -brotherhood-draft-platform-parliament.

32. Arab American Institute, "Arab Attitudes: 2011," July 2011, http://www .aaiusa.org/reports/arab-attitutes-2011.

CHAPTER THREE: THE WAHHABI COUNTERREVOLUTION

1. Jean-Francois Seznec, "Foreign Policy: Bahrain Spells Trouble for US Policy," February 18, 2011, http://www.npr.org/2011/02/18/133861647 /foreign-policy-bahrain-spells-trouble-for-us-policy.

2. Associated Press, "Iranian Commander Warns Saudi of Domestic Unrest," May 1, 2011, http://www.boston.com/news/world/middleeast/articles /2011/05/01/iranian_commander_warns_saudi_of_deployment_risk/.

3. Fars News Agency (Iran), "Spokesman Blasts Clinton's Controversial Claims About Iran," March 21, 2011, http://english.farsnews.com/news text.php?nn=9001010152.

4. Marc Lynch, "Tunisia's New Al-Nahda," *Foreign Policy,* June 29, 2011, http://lynch.foreignpolicy.com/posts/2011/06/29/tunisias_new_al_nahda.

5. Osama El-Mahdy, "Shias Accuse Saudi Arabia of Mobilizing Salafis to Disrupt Egypt's Unity," *Al-Masry Al-Youm,* April 10, 2011, http://www .almasryalyoum.com/en/node/393693; Osama Al-Mahdy, "Protest Before Saudi Embassy Against Financing Salafis," *Al-Masry Al-Youm,* May 17, 2011, http://www.almasryalyoum.com/en/node/440967.

6. *Al-Masry Al-Youm* (Cairo), "Saudi Minister Threatens to Expel Foreign Laborers, Egyptians Included," May 30, 2011, http://www.almasry alyoum.com/en/node/457639.

7. Reuters, "Saudi Handout Unlikely to Fuel Inflation, Says Official," March 25, 2011, http://www.thepeninsulaqatar.com/business-news/146740-saudi -handout-unlikely-to-fuel-inflation-says-official.html.

8. Glen Carey, "Saudi Arabia Defies Turmoil as Guardian of Status Quo," Bloomberg, May 18, 2011, http://www.bloomberg.com/news/2011-05-17 /saudi-arabia-defies-mideast-upheaval.html.

9. Declan Walsh, "Faith, Charity, and the Money Trail to Pakistan's Islamist Militants," *The Guardian* (London), August 21, 2007, http://www .guardian.co.uk/world/2007/aug/21/pakistan.declanwalsh; idem.; "Saudi Arabian Charity in Pakistan Offers Education—Or Is It Extremism?," *The Guardian* (London), June 29, 2011, http://www.guardian.co.uk /world/2011/jun/29/saudi-charity-pakistan-extremism.

10. Brian M. Downing, "Pakistan Marches to Saudi Tune," *Asia Times Online,* June 3, 2011, http://www.atimes.com/atimes/Middle_East/MF03Ak02.html.

11. Martin Walker, "Money and the Arab Spring," United Press International, May 31, 2011, http://www.upi.com/Top_News/Analysis/Walker /2011/05/31/Walkers-World-Money-and-the-Arab-Spring/UPI-7085130 6838220/#ixzz1O6XBZOw0.

12. Jamie Doward and Phillipa Stewart, "U.K. Training Saudi Forces Used to Crush Arab Spring," *The Guardian* (London), May 28, 2011, http://www .guardian.co.uk/world/2011/may/28/uk-training-saudi-troops.

13. Susan B. Glasser, "'Martyrs' in Iraq Mostly Saudis," *Washington Post,* May 15, 2005, http://www.washingtonpost.com/wp-dyn/content/article /2005/05/14/AR2005051401270.html.

14. Muhammed Al-Salami, "Kingdom Amends Media Laws," *Arab News* (Saudi Arabia), April 29, 2011, http://www.arabnews.com/saudiarabia /article377672.ece.

15. Neil MacFarquhar, "Saudi Arabia Scrambles to Limit Region's Upheaval," *New York Times,* May 27, 2011, http://www.nytimes.com/2011/05/28 /world/middleeast/28saudi.html?_r=2.

16. For more on this trip, see John R. Bradley, *Saudi Arabia Exposed: Inside a Kingdom in Crisis* (New York: Palgrave Macmillan, 2005), pp. 53-65.

17. Monia Ghanmi, "Tribalism Yields to Solidarity in Tunisia," *Magharebia .com,* July 20, 2011, http://www.magharebia.com/cocoon/awi/xhtml1/en _GB/features/awi/reportage/2011/05/20/reportage-01.

18. Ibid.

19. Ujala Sehgal, "How the U.S. Came to Negotiate With the Taliban," *Atlantic,* July 18, 2011, http://www.theatlanticwire.com/global/2011/06 /why-us-now-negotiating-taliban/38972/.

20. Annie Gowen and Asaad Majeed, "Attacks Across Iraq Kill More Than Eighty," *Washington Post,* August 15, 2011, http://www.washington post.com/world/middle-east/more-than-70-killed-in-attacks-across-iraq /2011/08/15/gIQAHYtWGJ_story.html.

21. *BBC News Online,* "August Was 'Deadliest Month' for U.S. in Afghan War," August 30, 2011, http://www.bbc.co.uk/news/world-us-canada -14720918.

22. Associated Press, "Yemen Tribe Turns Guns Against Saleh," May 24, 2011, http://www.huffingtonpost.com/2011/05/24/yemen-tribe-ali-abdullah -saleh_n_866139.html; http://www.telegraph.co.uk/news/worldnews/mid dleeast/yemen/8499162/Yemen-Ali-Abdullah-Saleh-vows-to-cling-to -power.html; Adrian Blomfield, "Yemen: Ali Abdullah Saleh Vows to Cling to Power," *The Telegraph* (London), May 6, 2011, http://www.telegraph .co.uk/news/worldnews/middleeast/yemen/8499162/Yemen-Ali -Abdullah-Saleh-vows-to-cling-to-power.html.

23. Hakim Almasmari, "Yemen Claims Opposition Figures Behind Assassination Attempt," CNN, August 19, 2011, http://edition.cnn.com/2011 /WORLD/meast/08/19/yemen.charges/.

24. United Press International, "Trial of Yemen Al-Qaeda No. 2 Ends, Verdict on April 26," April 18, 2006, http://www.monstersandcritics .com/news/middleeast/news/article_1156279.php/Trial_of_Yemen_al -Qaeda_No_2_ends_verdict_on_April_26.

25. Michel Cousins, "Kingdom-Yemen Emergency Talks Set Over Border Fence," *Arab News* (Saudi Arabia), February 10, 2004, http://archive .arabnews.com/?page=1&section=0&article=39304&d=10&m= 2&y=2004.

26. For more on this trip, see: John R. Bradley, "Bad Fences," *New Republic,* March 1, 2004, http://www.tnr.com/article/bad-fences.

27. Ibid.

28. Jeb Boone, "Yemen's Saleh Cedes Al-Qaeda Hotbed to Militants. Why?," *Christian Science Monitor,* May 31, 2011, http://www.csmonitor.com /World/Middle-East/2011/0531/Yemen-s-Saleh-cedes-Al-Qaeda-hotbed -to-militants.-Why; "Al-Qaida Seizes Another Large City in Southeast Yemen," Xinhua News Agency, June 2, 2011, http://news.xinhuanet.com /english2010/world/2011-06/02/c_13906217.htm.

29. SABA News Agency (Yemen), "Yemeni Official Warns of Civil War," August 20, 2011, http://www.sabanews.net/en/news246340.htm.

30. Agence-France Presse, "Yemen Qaeda Cuts off Boy's Hand," September 9, 2011, http://www.news24.com/World/News/Yemen-Qaeda-cuts -off-boys-hand-20110925.

31. Bradley, "Bad Fences."

32. Frank Gardner, "Yemen's New Anti-Terror Strategy," *BBC News Online,* December 16, 2003, http://news.bbc.co.uk/2/hi/middle_east/3326121 .stm.

33. "Urgent Statement by the Leadership of the Southern Democratic Assembly (TAJ-South Yemen) to the International Community," November 30, 2005, http://www.soutalgnoub.com/data29.htm.

34. Giles Foden, "Ace of Base," *The Guardian* (London), November 18, 2003, http://www.guardian.co.uk/world/2003/nov/18/turkey.alqaida1.

35. Nicholas Blanford, "Are Iran and Al-Qaeda Vying for Influence in Yemen?," *Christian Science Monitor,* July 13, 2004, http://www.csmonitor .com/2004/0713/p11s01-wome.html.

36. *BBC News Online,* "'Net Closes' Around Yemen Rebels," July 5, 2004, http://news.bbc.co.uk/2/hi/middle_east/3868221.stm.

37. Associated Press, "U.S. Imam Wanted in Yemen Over Al-Qaeda Suspicions," November 11, 2009, http://www.asharq-e.com/news.asp?section =1&id=18774.

38. Ginny Hill, "Yemen Divided on Vice and Virtue," *BBC News Online,* August 11, 2008, http://news.bbc.co.uk/2/hi/7546907.stm.

39. Iona Craig and Tom Coghlan, "Arab Spring Reaches Full Bloom," *The Times* (London), June 7, 2011, http://www.theaustralian.com.au/news /features/arab-spring-reaches-full-bloom/story-e6frg6z6-1226070465743.

40. Jeb Boone, "Yemen's Protests Hijacked: Yemen's Youth Have Lost Control of the Revolution They Began," *Global Post,* July 3, 2011, http://www.globalpost.com/dispatch/news/regions/middle-east/110702 /yemen-protests-hijacked.

41. Xinhua News Agency (China), "Twenty-three Yemeni Opposition Leaders Withdraw From National Council," August 20, 2011, http://news.xinhua net.com/english2010/world/2011-08/20/c_131062174.htm.

42. Pepe Escobar, "Exposed: The US-Saudi Libya Deal," *Asia Times Online,* April 2, 2011, http://www.atimes.com/atimes/Middle_East/MD02Ak01 .html.

43. Ibid.

44. David D. Kirkpatrick, "Libya Allying With Islamists, Qaddafi Son Says," *New York Times,* August 3, 2011, http://www.nytimes.com/2011/08/04 /world/africa/04seif.html?pagewanted=all.

45. *Strafor,* "Libya's Opposition Leadership Comes Into Focus," March 20, 2011, http://www.stratfor.com/analysis/20110307-libyas-opposition-lead ership-comes-focus.

46. David D. Kirkpatrick, "Hopes for a Qaddafi Exit, and Worries of What Comes Next," *New York Times,* March 21, 2011, http://www.nytimes .com/2011/03/22/world/africa/22tripoli.html?_r=3&hp.

47. Charles Levinson, "Ex-Mujahedeen Help Lead Libyan Rebels," *Wall Street Journal,* April 2, 2011, http://online.wsj.com/article/SB100014240 52748703712504576237042432212406.html.

48. *Washington Times,* "Topic: Libyan Islamic Fighting Group," undated, http://www.washingtontimes.com/topics/libyan-islamic-fighting -group/.

49. Deutsche Welle (Germany), "Libyan Islamists Stand to Gain With or Without Gadhafi," March 24, 2011, http://www.dw-world.de/dw /article/0,14934994,00.html.

50. Praveen Swami, "Libyan Rebel Commander Admits His Fighters Have Al-Qaeda Links," *The Telegraph* (London), March 25, 2011, http://www .telegraph.co.uk/news/worldnews/africaandindianocean/libya/84070 47/Libyan-rebel-commander-admits-his-fighters-have-al-Qaeda-links .html.

51. *France-24,* "Shifting Loyalties Among Libya's Islamists," August 10, 2011, http://www.france24.com/en/20110805-libya-uprising-islamists-re bels-ntc-gaddafi-fighters-transition-council-shifting-allies; Lindsey Hilsum, "Meeting the Families Left Behind by Gaddafi's Prison Massacre," Channel 4 News (U.K.), http://blogs.channel4.com/world-news-blog /meeting-the-families-left-behind-by-gaddafis-prison-massacre/15306.

52. Gamal Nkrumah, "Benghazi Nears the Brink?," *Al-Ahram Weekly Online* (Egypt), March 17-23, 2011, http://weekly.ahram.org.eg/2011/1039/re1.htm.

53. Christiane Amanpour, "'My People Love Me': Muammar Gaddafi Denies Demonstrations Against Him Anywhere in Libya," ABC News, February 28, 2011, http://abcnews.go.com/International/christiane -amanpour-interviews-libyas-moammar-gadhafi/story?id=13019942.

54. Richard Spencer, "Libya: The West and Al-Qaeda on the Same Side," *The Telegraph* (London), March 18, 2011, http://www.telegraph.co.uk/news /worldnews/africaandindianocean/libya/8391632/Libya-the-West-and-al -Qaeda-on-the-same-side.html.

55. *The National* (Abu Dhabi), "Tribe of Murdered Libyan General Promises It Will Seek Justice for His Death," August 4, 2011, http://www .thenational.ae/news/worldwide/africa/tribe-of-murdered-libyan-general -promises-it-will-seek-justice-for-his-death.

56. George Friedman, "Re-examining the Arab Spring," *Stratfor,* August 15, 2011, http://www.stratfor.com/weekly/20110815-re-examining-arab -spring.

57. Associated Press, Dario Lopez and Karin Laub, "Libyan Rebels Say They Are Attacking Tripoli," August 20, 2011, http://www.kansascity .com/2011/08/20/3088727/libyan-rebels-say-they-are-attacking.html.

58. Lisa Karpova, "NATO War Crimes, the Murder of Journalists," *Pravda .com,* August 3, 2011, http://english.pravda.ru/opinion/columnists/03-08 -2011/118651-NATO_war_crimes_murder_of_journalists-0/.

59. One such rally in July 2011 can be seen here: http://www.youtube.com /watch?v=jWzNhk3zv4U.

60. Jonathan Brown, "Rebels Claim Victory—But Did the Brits Win It?," *The Independent* (U.K.), August 23, 2011, http://www.independent.co.uk /news/world/africa/rebels-claim-the-victory-ndash-but-did-the-brits-win -it-2342152.html; Barbara Starr, "Foreign Forces in Libya Helping Rebel Forces Advance," CNN, August 24, 2011, http://edition.cnn.com/2011 /WORLD/africa/08/24/libya.foreign.forces/.

61. Klifford Krauss, "The Scramble for Access to Libya's Oil Wealth Begins," *New York Times,* August 22, 2011, http://www.nytimes.com/2011/08/23 /business/global/the-scramble-for-access-to-libyas-oil-wealth-begins.html.

62. Charles Levinson, "Minister in Tripoli Blasts Qatari Aid to Militia Groups," *Wall Street Journal,* October 12, 2011, http://online.wsj.com /article/SB10001424052970203499704576625441762600166.html.

63. Stephen J. Sniegoski, *The Transparent Cabal: The Neoconservative Agenda, War in the Middle East, and the National Interest of Israel* (Norfolk, Virginia: IHS Press, 2008).

64. "Libya: Draft Constitutional Charter for the Transitional Stage," https: //www.documentcloud.org/documents/238344-libya-draft-constitutional -charter-for-the.html.

CHAPTER FOUR: THE SHIA AXIS

1. "Geopolitically Strategic Yemen Has Become a Focus of Local Iranian-Saudi Arabian Strife," *terrorism-info.org,* October 1, 2009, http://www .terrorism-info.org.il/malam_multimedia/English/eng_n/html/iran_e025 .htm; *Stratfor,* "Iran: A Naval Deployment and the Houthi Rebellion," November 16, 2009, http://www.stratfor.com/memberships/148952/analy sis/20091116_iran_naval_deployment_and_houthi_rebellion.

2. See Joshua Teitelbaum's classic study, *Holier Than Thou: Saudi Arabia's Islamic Opposition* (Washington, DC: Washington Institute for Near East Policy, 2000).

3. Jay Solomon, "Challenger Mousavi Has Conservative Past," *Wall Street Journal,* June 17, 2009, http://online.wsj.com/article/SB1245196 76619521077.html.

4. Adam Rozell and Jishua Haber, "Confront the Saudis for Teaching Hate," *New York Post,* July 2, 2008, http://www.nypost.com/p/news/opinion /opedcolumnists/confront_the_saudis_for_teaching_wPPh0MRumWp IxK2d9k7R2I; http://www.nypost.com/p/news/opinion/opedcolumnists /confront_the_saudis_for_teaching_wPPh0MRumWpIxK2d9k7R2I.

5. David Amess, "Arab Spring Needs Iranian Summer to Survive," United Press International, July 6, 2011, http://www.upi.com/Top_News /Analysis/Outside-View/2011/07/06/Outside-View-Arab-Spring-needs -Iranian-Summer-to-survive/UPI-10751309954560/#ixzz1UtvyniR4.

6. Anthony Shadid, "A Syrian Beacon Pays Price for Its Dissent," *New York Times,* April 27, 2011, http://www.nytimes.com/2011/04/28/world/middleeast/28daraa.html?pagewanted=all.

7. Ryan Mauro, "The Mullah's Rescue Assad," *FrontPage Magazine,* April 13, 2011, http://frontpagemag.com/2011/04/13/iran-comes-to-assad%E2%80%99s-rescue/.

8. Reuters, "Tehran Ready to Give Syria $5.8 Billion: Report," July 15, 2011, http://www.reuters.com/article/2011/07/15/us-syria-iran-idUSTRE76E3C720110715.

9. Ibid.

10. Reuters, "Turkey Says It Seized Illegal Iran Arms Shipment," March 31, 2011, http://www.newsmax.com/Newsfront/Turkey-Iran-arms-seized/2011/03/31/id/391351.

11. Natacha Yazbeck, "Hezbollah Urges Syrians to Back Assad Regime," Agence France-Presse, May 25, 2011, http://www.google.com/hostednews/afp/article/ALeqM5jFv4_d9yBq5WmgGkDd0_VttkWPTg?docId=CNG.6d368e1b8c6c3ad77e8681f96fb6d5ee.301.

12. For more on socially liberal Damascus, see ch. 1, "Dissent in Damascus," in John R. Bradley, *Behind the Veil of Vice: The Business and Culture of Sex in the Middle East* (New York: Palgrave Macmillan, 2010).

13. These are my personal observations from a visit to Syria in 2008. For a report on how the number of Syrian women who don the veil and *niqab* has increased in the recent years, and how this led to the initial ban in schools and universities, see: Robert Weller, "Syria Bans Female Teachers From Wearing Veils," *Huffington Post,* June 30, 2010, http://www.huffingtonpost.com/robert-weller/syria-bans-female-teacher_b_630134.html.

14. Associated Press, "Syria Relaxes Veil Ban for Teachers," April 6, 2011, http://www.guardian.co.uk/world/2011/apr/06/syria-relax-veil-ban-teacher.

15. *Ynetnews* (Israel), "Syria: Prisoners Freed, Protesters Arrested," March 26, 2011, http://www.ynetnews.com/articles/0,7340,L-4047912,00.html.

16. United Press International, "Observers: Protests Could Turn Sectarian," July 19, 2011, http://www.upi.com/Top_News/World-News/2011/07/19/Observers-Protests-could-turn-sectarian/UPI-39481311075233/#ixzz1V4uTKvQT.

17. Zaid Abu Fadel, "Sectarianism Dominates the Movement Against Syria's Government," *Arab-American News,* July 25, 2011, http://www.arab

americannews.com/news/index.php?mod=article&cat=ArabWorld&
article=4398.

18. Ibid. See also Adrian Blomfield, "Syrian Opposition Admits Armed Insurgents Are Operating on Fringe of Uprising Against Assad Regime," *The Telegraph* (London), August 6, 2011, http://www.telegraph.co.uk /news/8686582/Syrian-opposition-admits-armed-insurgents-are -operating-on-fringe-of-uprising-against-Assad-regime.html.

19. *RTTNews,* "Massive Pro-Govt. Rallies in Syria as Assad Orders New Amnesty," June 21, 2011, http://www.rttnews.com/Content/PoliticalNews .aspx?Id=1650686&SM=1.

20. *Al-Jazeera English,* "Saudi Arabia Calls for Syrian Reforms," August 8, 2011, http://english.aljazeera.net/news/middleeast/2011/08/20118721392 2184761.html.

21. Martin Chulov, "Syria: Assad Must Resign, Says Obama," *The Guardian* (London), August 19, 2011, http://www.guardian.co.uk/world/2011 /aug/18/syria-assad-must-resign-obama.

22. Nour Ali, "Defiant Assad Addresses Syria on TV as U.N. Arrives in Damascus," *The Guardian* (London), August 22, 2011, http://www.guardian .co.uk/world/2011/aug/21/syrian-president-assad-addresses-nation.

23. Oren Kessler, "Religion—The Overlooked Motive Behind Syria's Uprising," *Jerusalem Post,* May 20, 2011, http://www.jpost.com/Features /InThespotlight/Article.aspx?id=221408.

24. Some of the material on Iran's ethnic groups contained in this chapter first appeared in a different form as part of a longer essay I wrote on the subject for *The Washington Quarterly.* See John R. Bradley, "Iran's Ethnic Tinderbox," *The Washington Quarterly* 30:1 (Winter 2006-07): 181–190, © 2006-07 by The Center for Strategic and International Studies and the Massachusetts Institute of Technology, www.tandfonline.com. Reprinted with permission.

25. Brenda Shaffer, "Iran's Volatile Ethnic Mix," *International Herald Tribune,* June 2, 2006, http://www.iht.com/articles/2006/06/02/opinion /edshaffer.php.

26. Guy Dinmore, "U.S. Marines Probe Tensions Among Iran's Minorities," *Financial Times,* February 24, 2006, p. 2.

27. Seymour M. Hersh, "The Iran Plans," *New Yorker,* April 17, 2006, p. 30.

28. Dinmore, "U.S. Marines Probe Tensions."

29. Amir Taheri, "Iran: Ethnic Woes," *New York Sun,* February 6, 2006, http: //www.benadorassociates.com/article/19305.

30. Abbas William Samii, "Ethnic Tensions Could Crack Iran's Firm Resolve Against the World," *Christian Science Monitor,* May 30, 2006, http://www.csmonitor.com/2006/0530/p09s02-coop.html.

31. Associated Press, "Iran's President: U.S. Will Fail to Provoke Ethnic Differences," May 24, 2006.

32. Associated Press, "Iran Blames U.K. for Bombings," January 25, 2008, http://www.usatoday.com/news/world/2006-01-25-iranbombings_x.htm.

33. *British Ahwazi Friendship Society,* "Iran: Parliamentary Think Tank Warns of Ethnic Unrest," January 5, 2006.

34. "Ahwazi: Iranian Regime Has Killed Thousands of Ahwazis," July 20, 2011, *Asharq Al-Awsat,* http://www.unpo.org/article/12925.

35. Residents of Khuzestan, interviews with author, March 2006. The villagers asked that their names not be used and the location of their village not be specified.

36. Amnesty International, "Iran: Need for Restraint as Anniversary of Unrest in Khuzestan Approaches," April 13, 2006, http://web.amnesty.org/library/Index/ENGMDE130402006?open&of=ENG-IRN.

37. *BBC News Online,* "Iran Bans Al-Jazeera After Riots," April 19, 2005, http://news.bbc.co.uk/2/hi/middle_east/4459033.stm.

38. John R. Bradley, "Ethnicity Versus Theocracy," *Al-Ahram Weekly* (Egypt), March 16, 2006, http://weekly.ahram.org.eg/2006/786/re7.htm.

39. Ibid.

40. Ibid.

41. Associated Press, "Al-Qaeda Leader Urges Attacks on Gulf Oil Facilities," December 7, 2005, http://www.rferl.org/featuresarticle/2005/12/3c997d85-35f1-4854-9eec-ccd483c981ef.html.

42. Taheri, "Iran: Ethnic Woes."

CHAPTER FIVE: LESSONS FROM SOUTHEAST ASIA

1. Peter Boyle, "Malaysia: 'Politics Has Become More Dangerous,'" *Green Left Review,* July 10, 2011, http://www.greenleft.org.au/node/48117.

2. John Mintz and Douglas Farah, "In Search of Friends Among the Foes," *Washington Post,* September 11, 2004, http://www.washingtonpost.com/ac2/wp-dyn/A12823-2004Sep10?language=printer. See also Seth Mandel, "A Primer on the International Institute of Islamic Thought: The Terror-Supporting Intellectual Façade of the Muslim Brotherhood," *NewsReelBlog,*

January 28, 2011, http://www.newsrealblog.com/2011/01/28/a-primer-on-the-international-institute-of-islamic-thought-the-terror-supporting-intellectual-facade-of-the-muslim-brotherhood/.

3. *BBC News Online,* "Profile: Mahathir Mohamad," October 31, 2003, http://news.bbc.co.uk/2/hi/asia-pacific/2059518.stm.

4. Richard Lloyd Parry, "Attacks After Malaysian Court Rules Christians Can Worship Allah," *The Times* (London), January 9, 2010, http://www.timesonline.co.uk/tol/news/world/asia/article6980360.ece.

5. Bernama News Agency (Malaysia), "Bernama Journalist's Account of Bersih Rally," July 31, 2011, http://www.malaysiandigest.com/features/28251-bernama-journalists-accounts-of-bersih-rally.html.

6. Michael Jansen, "Saudis Trying to Choke Arab Spring," *Irish Times,* June 1, 2011, http://www.irishtimes.com/newspaper/world/2011/0601/1224298205470.html.

7. Martin van Bruinessen, "Wahhabi Influences in Indonesia, Real and Imagined." Summary of a paper presented at the Journée d'Etudes du CEIFR et MSH sur le Wahhabisme (2002), http://www.let.uu.nl/~martin.van bruinessen/personal/publications/Wahhabi%20influences%20in%20 Indonesia.htm.

8. The information contained in this section on southern Thailand is drawn from a dispatch I wrote based on a monthlong trip to the region in 2004. See John R. Bradley, "Waking Up to the Terror Threat in Southern Thailand," *Straits Times* (Singapore), May 27, 2004, http://yaleglobal.yale.edu/content/waking-terror-threat-southern-thailand.

9. *BBC News One,* "Thai Mosque Killings Criticised," July 28, 2004, http://news.bbc.co.uk/2/hi/asia-pacific/3932323.stm.

10. Tyrell Haberkorn, "In Bangkok: Remembering the Tak Bai Massacre," *OpenDemocracy.net,* November 3, 2009, http://www.opendemocracy.net/tyrell-haberkorn/in-bangkok-remembering-tak-bai-massacre.

11. Ron Corben, "Disappearance of Thai Lawyer Still Not Solved," *Asia Calling* (Thailand), March 26, 2011, http://www.asiacalling.org/en/news/thailand/1932-disappearance-of-thai-lawyer-still-not-solved.

12. Country Studies, "Pancasila," http://countrystudies.us/indonesia/86.htm.

13. Sholto Byrnes, "One Nation Undivided Under God," *New Statesman* (U.K.), August 9, 2010, http://www.newstatesman.com/asia/2010/08/indonesia-muslim-suharto-east.

14. Ibid.

15. Bruinessen, "Wahhabi Influences in Indonesia."

16. Simon Montlake, "In Indonesian Election, Secular Parties Confirm Appeal," *Christian Science Monitor,* April 9, 2009, http://www.csmonitor.com/World/Asia-Pacific/2009/0409/p06s10-woap.html.

17. Bruinessen, "Wahhabi Influences in Indonesia."

18. International Crisis Group, "Indonesia: 'Christianisation' and Intolerance," November 24, 2010, http://www.crisisgroup.org/en/regions/asia/south-east-asia/indonesia/B114-indonesia-christianisation-and-intolerance.aspx.

19. Dr. Adam Burke shared his personal experience of peace building in Aceh in the years after the Asian tsunami through a researcher for this book.

20. Karishma Vaswani, "On Patrol With Aceh's Sharia Police," *BBC News Online,* February 2, 2010, http://news.bbc.co.uk/2/hi/asia-pacific/8491195.stm.

21. Papenidea, "History of Aceh, the Veranda of Mecca," http://papanidea.com/2011/07/history-of-aceh-the-veranda-of-mecca/.

22. Al Islam: The Official Site of the Ahmadiyya Muslim Community, "The Promised Messiah, a Prophet to Unite Mankind in the Latter Days," http://www.alislam.org/topics/messiah/index.php.

23. International Crisis Group, "Indonesia: Implications of the Ahmadiyah Decree," July 7, 2008, http://www.unhcr.org/refworld/docid/4872251e2.html.

24. "Joint Decree of the Minister of Religious Affairs, the Attorney General and the Minister of the Interior of the Republic of Indonesia," reprinted by *The Persecution: Religious Persecution of the Ahmadiyya Muslim Community,* 2006, http://www.thepersecution.org/world/indonesia/docs/skb.html.

25. International Crisis Group, "Indonesia: Implications of the Ahmadiyah Decree."

26. Lee Hudson Teslik, "Profile: Abu Bakar Bashir," *Council on Foreign Relations,* June 14, 2006, http://www.cfr.org/indonesia/profile-abu-bakar-bashir-k-baasyir/p10219.

27. Australian Associated Press, "CIA Used 'Micro Nuclear' Bomb in Bali: Bashir," August 29, 2006, http://www.smh.com.au/news/world/bashir-blames-bali-on-cia-bomb/2006/08/29/1156816891620.html.

28. Scot Atran, "The Emir: An Interview with Abu Bakar Bashir, Alleged Leader of the Southeast Asian Jemaah Islamiyah Organization," *Jamestown*

Foundation, December 16, 2005, http://www.jamestown.org/programs /gta/single/?tx_ttnews[tt_news]=562&tx_ttnews[backPid]=26&cHash =f0e77f13a0.

29. Farah Stockman, "Cleric's Trial Tests U.S. Anti-Terror Fight," *Boston Globe,* March 2, 2005, http://www.boston.com/news/nation /articles/2005/03/02/clerics_trial_tests_us_antiterror_fight/.

30. Evan Williams, "Hamzah Haz Interview Transcript," *Australian Broadcasting Corporation,* October 23, 2010, http://www.abc.net.au/foreign /stories/s710402.htm.

31. Brad Nelson and Yohanes Sulaiman, "Bashir's Downfall Reflects Waning Influence of Radicals," *Jakarta Post,* June 30, 2011, http://www.thejakartaglobe.com/opinion/bashirs-downfall-reflects -waning-influence-of-radicals/449753.

32. Heru Andriyanto, "Judgment Day for Bashir in Terror Trial," *Jakarta Post,* June 16, 2011, http://www.thejakartaglobe.com/indonesia /judgment-day-for-bashir-in-terror-trial/447214.

33. Indonesia Matters, "Wahabi & Wahhabism," November 11, 2008, http: //www.indonesiamatters.com/1610/wahabi-wahhabism/.

34. Byrnes, "One Nation Undivided Under God."

35. *BBC News Online,* "Competing Muslim Brotherhood Visions for Egypt," March 3, 2011, http://news.bbc.co.uk/2/hi/programmes/news night/9412967.stm.

36. Jennifer Pak, "Rise of Strict Islam Exposes Tensions in Malaysia," *BBC News Online,* August 26, 2011, http://www.bbc.co.uk/news /world-radio-and-tv-14649841.

CHAPTER SIX: WHAT NEXT?

1. Max Boot, "Are We All Neocons Now?," *Commentary,* January 28, 2011, http://www.commentarymagazine.com/2011/01/28/are-we-all-neocons -now/.

2. Hassane Zerrouky, "The Future of Arab Revolts: Interview with Samir Amin," *Monthly Review,* August 11, 2011, http://mrzine.monthlyreview .org/2011/amin110811.html.

3. Shadi Hamid, "How Islamists Will Change Politics, and Vice Versa," *Foreign Affairs,* May/June 2011, http://www.foreignaffairs.com /articles/67696/shadi-hamid/the-rise-of-the-islamists.

4. Bruce Thornton, "Liberating Libya for Jihadists," *FrontPageMag .com,* August 30, 2011, http://frontpagemag.com/2011/08/30/liberating -libya-for-jihadists/2/.

5. Andrés Cala, "Inspired by Arab Spring, Spain's Youthful 15-M Movement Spreads in Europe," *Christian Science Monitor,* May 20, 2011, http: //www.csmonitor.com/World/Europe/2011/0520/Inspired-by-Arab-Spring -Spain-s-youthful-15-M-movement-spreads-in-Europe.

6. AlifArabia.com, "Arab Spring in America?," August 21, 2011, http://alif arabia.com/2011/08/21/an-arab-spring-in-the-united-states/.

7. John-Paul Ford Rojas, "London Riots: Lidl Water Thief Jailed for Six Months," *The Telegraph* (London), August 11, 2011, http://www.telegraph .co.uk/news/uknews/crime/8695988/London-riots-Lidl-water-thief-jailed -for-six-months.html.

8. *Alex Jones Show,* "Ron Paul: Rick Perry Is the Globalist Choice for 2012," Interview, August 31, 2011, http://www.youtube.com/watch ?feature=player_embedded&v=Qfni3McvYns.

9. John Lanchester, "The Non-Scenic Route to the Place We're Going Anyway," *London Review of Books,* September 8, 2011, http://www.lrb.co.uk/v33 /n17/john-lanchester/the-non-scenic-route-to-the-place-were-going -anyway.

INDEX